PRAISE FOR *STRAIGHT SHOOTING: A WORLD CHAMPION'S GUIDE TO SHOTGUNNING*

"If you are going to get one book on how to shoot sporting clays, *Straight Shooting* is it."

—Bruce Buck, *Shooting Sportsman*

"It's accessible, easy to reference, and packed full of knowledge. Seriously, the depth of information is truly astounding."

—Dominic Grossi, *Shotgun Sports*

"A must-have guide for serious shotgunners."

—Dana Farrell, *Shooting Sports USA*

"Matarese completely dissects the sport down to the molecular level, and given his grasp of the topic, one could figure he's forgotten more about the sport than most have ever learned."

—John Petrolino, *Bearing Arms*

STRAIGHT SHOOTING
FOR HUNTERS

STRAIGHT SHOOTING
FOR HUNTERS

A Champion's Guide to Using Shotguns in the Field

Anthony I. Matarese Jr. and Will Primos

WITH **KERRY LUFT**

Published by A.I.M. Shooting School Press, Pennsville, New Jersey
clayshootinginstruction.com

Edited and designed by Girl Friday Productions
www.girlfridayproductions.com

Design: Paul Barrett
Project management: Sara Addicott
Editorial production: Katherine Richards

Principal photography by Trevor Shannahan. Additional photography by Thaddius Bedford and from Matarese and Primos family collections.

ISBN (paperback): 978-1-7373304-1-7
ISBN (ebook): 978-1-7373304-2-4
ISBN (audiobook): 978-1-7373304-3-1

Library of Congress Control Number: 2024912768

First edition

CONTENTS

FOREWORD

Few experiences stir the soul as profoundly as a grouse darting through aspen groves ahead of a poised pointer or a flock of mallards gracefully descending into decoys on a crisp autumn morning. For many of us, our spirits remain tethered to these moments as we long for the next return to the wilds that make us feel vibrantly alive. At onX Hunt, our mission is dedicated to guiding you to such havens, be they nestled in remote corners of the nation or a mere stone's throw from your home, and we are thrilled to announce our collaboration with *Straight Shooting for Hunters*.

In the quest for wild game, mastering the variables becomes essential, given the precious nature of both time and opportunity. With access to more than 852 million acres of public land and 147 million private properties through our app, you'll avoid the frustration of scouring barren lands or battling for access. Our maps will help you find optimal hunting spots, but once you're there, the outcome rests on you and your trusted shotgun. And that's where Primos and Matarese can help.

Will Primos, a figure synonymous with hunting and an earnest scholar of the game he pursues, represents the epitome of dedication and skill. During a memorable trip to the rugged landscapes of southern Arizona in 2019, Will and I sought the elusive Montezuma quail. The challenging terrain and the birds' cunning defensive maneuvers initially bested him, but change was on the horizon. Will's ongoing commitment to excellence has led him to collaborate with leading figures in the shooting field, including Anthony Matarese Jr., the most lauded American sporting clays shooter and a renowned instructor. Their alliance brings together profound expertise and narratives, enriching this book with valuable insights and engaging stories.

onX Hunt is proud to support this partnership, and we hope that whether you are a seasoned hunter, a clay shooter eager to explore hunting, or someone new to the sport, this book will help you refine your skills in both locating and skillfully harvesting game.

Ben Brettingen
Wingshooting Manager
onX Hunt

ON ✕ **HUNT**

Ben Brettingen with his setter Fred.

INTRODUCTION

One's a compact, talkative Southerner who's never met a stranger. The other is a tall, quiet native of New Jersey. Superficialities aside, though, Will Primos and Anthony I. Matarese Jr. have more in common than you'd expect.

Both are at the pinnacle of their professions. Anthony is a world-class shotgun shooter, the first American to win both world sporting clays championships and the only person to win the sport's four biggest events: the world championship, the world FITASC championship, the national championship, and the U.S. Open. Will's one of the greatest innovators in the hunting industry, having designed and produced state-of-the-art game calls and other equipment for decades while pioneering hunting shows for television and home video.

Yet there are deeper similarities between these two gentlemen, qualities they bring to this book. A deep-seated belief in the value of hunting and its role in American culture. A conviction that anything worth doing is worth doing well. And an abiding faith in family, friends, and the connections made and the lessons learned during a lifetime in the field.

Listen to Will reminisce about his beloved father, who, shortly after returning from his service during World War II as a navigator on a B-24 bomber in the Pacific theater, took young Will, age six, on his first squirrel hunt. Or hear the tales about Will's uncle Gus, a master hunter who seemed to magically summon mallards from thin air and inspired Will to create his first duck call at age eleven. Take note of the pride in Anthony's voice when he talks about his grandparents, who opened a famous goose-hunting outfitting service in Delaware many years before he was born, or about his parents, who founded one of the nation's most successful hunting preserves and developed it into a mecca for clay target shooting.

That same pride is evident when Anthony talks today about hunting with his three young daughters and his plans to hunt with his infant son, or when Will relates his excitement about introducing a newcomer to turkey hunting or the magic of the flooded timber as the sun rises over the Mississippi delta.

Those sentiments, more than any other, are the reason why they wrote this book—to help you and others learn to have greater success in the hunting fields and, in turn, pass along that joy to others. Now sit back and get ready to learn from two of the masters in our sport.

WILL'S STORY

I hunted for almost sixty years before I realized I didn't know how to shoot a shotgun.

Don't get me wrong—when I went duck hunting in my favorite flooded-timber holes, I usually came back with a strap of mallards. I was a pretty good caller, I had good spots, and I knew how to hide. My buddies did, too, and when the mallards started spilling air toward our decoys, the shots were easy. We just pointed at their feet, pulled the trigger, and sent the dog on a retrieve.

Then one day, the wind forced us to set up differently in a duck hole—instead of the ducks coming right at our blind, the strong, cold, sleet-filled wind forced us to try to get them to cross from left to right in front of us. Usually, that's an effective setup because the ducks are looking at the decoys, not at your blind.

On the first flock of gadwalls, our plan worked like a charm. I picked out the lead drake, and I knew he was mine. I fired both barrels of my 16-gauge side-by-side. But he kept on flying, while my friends whooped and hollered. That set the tone for the morning. The gadwalls kept coming from left to right, and I kept missing. Eventually I scratched down a limit, but I also was scratching my head. What was wrong with me? Why couldn't I connect on a crossing shot, and why had it taken so many shells to fill a limit?

After all, I had been a marksmanship instructor in the United States Air Force, and years ago I won the Mississippi State skeet championship in the junior division (though I'll confess I was the only junior competitor). It couldn't be that I simply didn't know what I was doing . . . or could it?

Will won a skeet trophy as a junior—but he was the only competitor!

I decided that I had to get better and started shooting sporting clays, a game that was designed for hunters but has since become a popular game on its own. I took lessons from top-level instructors, including some national and world champions: John Woolley, Dale Bouchillon, Royce Murphy, Gebben and Karen Miles, Jimmy Grant, Kevin DeMichiel, Chad Johnston, and Bill McGuire. All of them helped me understand there's a big difference between aiming a shotgun and pointing it.

I kept practicing and kept getting better. Then, in 2022, I bought a book called *Straight Shooting: A World Champion's Guide to Shotgunning* by Anthony I. Matarese Jr. Everybody in sporting clays knows Anthony, the most accomplished American competitor in the sport's history. He's also the busiest instructor around. If you want a lesson, you must book him months in advance.

Anyway, his book was a revelation. I started taking it to the course and using it to learn how to break specific targets. I realized Anthony was an awesome teacher and instructor, and I also realized I could help him get his message to millions of hunters who rarely shoot clays but want to be a better shot.

I took a few hours of lessons from him. During the afternoon of the first day, I finally experienced the "magic" that great shooters describe. I set up for a target and called for it. When it came out, I swung with it, focusing on the little ring in its center and not worrying at all about getting out in front of it—giving it "lead," as most shooters would say. I pulled the trigger and smoked it.

They call such experiences aha moments. I called it a near miracle.

Since then, I've been working to get that feeling with every shot I take. It's happening more often, and I'm pretty sure it will keep getting better. I'm now seventy-two, and I feel like I'm a kid again.

This book is designed to help you feel that way, too. Anthony and I are both hunters at heart, and we want you to enjoy hunting as much as we do. I've always enjoyed it, but let me tell you . . . I think this duck season may be my best one yet. Gadwalls, look out!

ANTHONY'S STORY

I make my living shooting a shotgun and teaching other people how to shoot. It's in my blood.

My grandparents ran a waterfowl outfitting service in Smyrna, Delaware. My father, Anthony I. Matarese Sr., grew up in that environment. As a young man, he and my mother, Donna, moved across the Delaware River and started M&M Hunting in Pennsville, New Jersey.

A few years after that, I came along. By the time I was five or six years old, my dad had started me shooting, first with a BB gun, then a

.410 shotgun. I killed my first deer at age six, shooting slugs out of that .410, with my dad sitting at my side. Most of all, I loved to go waterfowl hunting with him, and chasing ducks and geese is a passion of mine to this day.

Around that same time, my parents heard about a new shooting game designed for hunters called sporting clays. It seemed like a good way to bring in more revenue, so in 1990, M&M put in its first course. I was six years old then, and I remember going out as we trained a crew of high school kids to throw targets. Later, I became a trapper myself—I was so small that I had to brace my feet against the trap to get enough leverage to cock the arm. And I loved to shoot.

My parents understood this, so they arranged for me to take lessons with Dan Carlisle, one of the greatest shooters in U.S. history—a national champion in sporting clays and an Olympic athlete in bunker trap and international skeet. By the time I was fifteen, I was competitive with the best shooters out there, and people started asking me for help. By the time I was a high school senior, I was teaching all day on Saturdays and Sundays and whenever I wanted after school.

Ultimately, I realized that teaching shooting would be my life's work—I enjoy it, I meet a lot of great people, I make a good living, and I get to work with my family. I live right next to M&M with my wife, Jessica; our three daughters, Emma, Amelia, and Madelyn; and our son, Anthony III.

I'm still competing in the biggest sporting clays tournaments, and in 2016, I became the first American to win the World Sporting Clays Championship at the E.J. Churchill Shooting Ground near London. In 2020, I added the World FITASC Championship, becoming the first person to win all four major titles: the World Sporting, the World FITASC, the U.S. National Championship, and the U.S. Open.

If it weren't for competition, I probably would never shoot another clay target—just some ducks and geese in the fall. Even then, I'm going to work to be the best shot I can be. There's nothing I take lightly (except maybe cooking). Some might consider this to be a personality flaw, and maybe it is. Yet my years of competing at the very highest level and teaching others how to shoot has convinced me that anything you want to do is worth doing well, even if it's only a pastime.

For Anthony, shooting, hunting, and fishing are family traditions.

That's why my friend Will Primos and I wrote this book. We want you to have more and better success in the hunting field, because shooting well is far more fun than shooting poorly. I know this book will help you become a better shooter and hunter, and I hope you enjoy reading it.

CHAPTER 1

WHAT IS GOOD SHOOTING?

If you visit Anthony's home range, M&M Hunting and Sporting Clays in Pennsville, New Jersey, you'll see a wall of evidence that he is the greatest sporting clays shooter in the history of the United States. Two world championship trophies. A national championship. Three U.S. Opens—and that's not counting his team world championships or the national and world titles he won as a junior shooter.

In the field, he proves that the old line about target shooters not being good hunters is ridiculous. In Argentina, he once decided to see if he could kill 100 doves with 100 shots. He did that four times in a single day. Yes, he missed a few—but then he waited for an opportunity to knock down a double with one shot, keeping his shell-to-bird ratio at an incredible 1 to 1. You don't want to bet against him in a duck blind, either.

Yet Anthony says he's not even the best shot in his own family. His younger brother, Mike, was a champion shooter himself, one of the best young talents the sport has seen. He decided he didn't like competition as much as Anthony, but he didn't hang up his shotgun. Mike is a fast, natural shot—likely to splash two ducks in the decoys while you're still lining up on your first bird. When the brothers hunt together, it's a good bet they'll take six birds out of one flock, with Mike shooting the closer birds while Anthony cleans up the back. Unless you've seen them in action, it's hard to explain just how good they are.

Yet one day not long ago, rough weather and tidal conditions forced the brothers to set up their decoys in a less-than-optimal spot on a big stretch of open water. The wind was howling at 30 miles an hour, stirring up whitecap waves, and the birds skirted the decoys at the limits of ethical shooting distance. On that day, in those conditions, two of the best shooters in the world and two other experienced hunters killed their limits . . . with two boxes of shells each. Was that bad shooting? Not in the slightest. Less-accomplished shots might not have killed any—and to be brutally honest, they probably shouldn't even try shots at that range under those conditions.

That's the first thing to understand about good shooting in the field. It's relative. Conditions play such a big role that it's nearly impossible to define good shooting simply by numbers.

Killing a limit of 12 or 15 doves with less than a box of shells on opening day is one thing; trying to do it a few weeks later with fewer easy shots is another. Over a point, a rooster pheasant can be easy pickings; one that surprises you by flushing at 35 yards is another matter entirely. Canada geese from pit blinds over decoys? It doesn't get much easier for waterfowlers. Pass-shooting them at 50 yards? Few hunters can do that consistently or ethically.

Many hunters judge shooting skill by the size of the bag. Got a limit? Then, by definition, many people think you're a good shot. But how many shells did you need to do it? What else was going on? And what other skills were involved?

What does that mean? Well, let's say you're a duck hunter. You have the following going for you:

- You have a good spot, with plenty of ducks around.
- The wind is perfect, coming from behind you at a steady 12 to 15 miles an hour.
- The sun is also at your back.
- You are concealed as well as possible, in a blind or in good cover.
- You and your buddy are expert duck callers, and you've set your decoys just right.
- Your retriever is energetic, experienced, and tenacious.

That's a recipe for an easy day of shooting. Odds are good that the mallards will decoy beautifully and you'll be shooting them at 25 yards or less. If you don't kill a duck cleanly, you've got a great dog to recover it. Take away one or two of those factors—say, you're not hidden well and the sun is lighting up your face like a moon pie—and the shooting's going to be a lot more challenging.

So let's agree on one characteristic of good hunters: They realize the game is about more than just shooting, and the better they are at addressing those other elements, the easier their shots become. A mediocre shot with an outstanding dog that puts up birds in good range is going to have a much easier time of it than a good shot with an uncontrollable dog!

Anthony's pet peeve in waterfowl hunting is when his blind companions aren't hidden correctly. Yes, he can kill birds cleanly at a longer distance than most and can shoot flaring birds to fill his limit. But as we said, it's not just about the shooting. Take the time to hide correctly— it will make you seem like a much better shot.

Let's look at another scenario, one that most hunters will probably recognize. A hunter takes a long poke at a goose and crumples it dead in the air. She counts off the distance as she walks out to pick up her prize—60 yards! The shot of a lifetime!

Does that achievement make this hunter a great shot? No, not unless she can do it again with a reasonable rate of success. Pulling off a difficult shot once is *luck*. Doing it repeatedly is *skill*.

Over the course of writing this book, we talked a lot about what constitutes good shooting. As we have discussed in this chapter, numbers are virtually meaningless because conditions vary so wildly. Besides, you probably shouldn't keep score when hunting, either.

But we agreed that the best hunters and shooters share some common ground:

- **They know their limits.** Anthony's comfortable with shots out to about 50 yards, and in some instances a bit farther. Will wants to get the birds within 40 yards.
- **They pick their shots.** They don't shoot at birds they hope to hit; they shoot at birds they *know* they can hit. Build your skill on the clays course, not on live birds.

- As part of that, **they know how to determine distances in the field**, quickly and accurately.
- **They pass up shots they struggle with**—even those that are easy for other shooters—then work to figure out how to do it better.
- **When they make a difficult shot, it's not luck.** They know they can do it again, at least most of the time.

Experience is a huge part of all this. Knowing when to stand up and shoot, how to read a flushing dog as it roots out game, and not getting flustered when an opportunity arises are skills developed only over time in the field. A book can help a little, but you've got to get out there and do it.

Where a book *can* help a great deal is with the shooting itself. Over the course of the next few chapters, we'll discuss the various categories of hunting with a shotgun: upland, doves, waterfowl, turkeys, and deer. We'll talk about our favorite gear for each, describe typical scenarios for hunting, suggest ways to make your shots easier, and—perhaps most important—suggest ways to practice your shooting on clay targets so that when hunting season rolls around, you'll be ready.

Hunting is almost always fun. But take it from us—it's more fun when you shoot well.

CHAPTER 2

BASICS OF SHOTGUN SHOOTING

We've all heard about the hunter who doesn't shoot clays but never misses birds, and we've also heard about the clay target champions who can't hit a bird to save their lives. We're still waiting to meet either one. Sure, there are successful hunters who put their duck guns away at the end of one season and don't pick them up till the next, just as there are clay shooters who have never gone into the field. But by and large, people who shoot with good fundamentals do well on the range and in the field.

That's why we've written this book: to walk you through the process that will make you a better and more successful hunter. Having trouble with certain shots? We hope to help you. If you always shoot limits, great! But maybe we can help you use fewer shells to do it. If you like to shoot clay targets—probably the best practice possible for hunting—this process will help you there as well.

To start with, we'll talk about the most fundamental parts of shooting a shotgun: how to point the gun, use your eyes properly, and establish a lead. Without an understanding of these concepts, we can't go any further.

Let's start with the biggest mistake almost everyone makes while shooting a shotgun: they tend to aim instead of "point." Many people have heard the concept of pointing a shotgun and aiming a rifle but don't fully understand it.

Think of the barrel/muzzle of your shotgun as similar to the hood of your car. You see it, but you're not looking at it. Instead, you look beyond the hood to a spot farther down the road. The barrel is used to help you steer, or point, your gun, but your eyes should be on your target. You'll know where the barrel is in relation to the bird, but you're not looking at it when you pull the trigger.

Other examples include hitting or catching a baseball. You don't look at the bat or the glove—you watch the ball, and your hands and eyes work together. Shooting a shotgun is very similar.

USING YOUR EYES

To understand the importance of vision, think of these scenarios:

1. **A bird surprises you.** You mount your gun at the last moment and fire, and the bird crumples. It's the best shot of the day, and not only are you surprised but so is everyone else.
2. **A goose locks up and sails straight into the decoys**—an absolute gimme. Three shots later, your Christmas dinner is still flying. Once again, you're surprised, but not in a good way.

In the first case, you relied on hand-eye coordination to make the shot. You had no time to look at the muzzle.

In the second, you had plenty of time to get ready—maybe too much time. The miss probably occurred because you looked at your barrel or tried to measure a lead without looking at a specific part of the bird. It happens to all of us.

Here's how to fix that: *Make sure the bird is in focus.*

For simplicity's sake, let's define "focus" as "seeing a part of the bird clearly when you pull the trigger." In other words, you need your eyes 100 percent locked on *a part* of the dove, duck, pheasant, or clay, and you will see the barrel or muzzle as a blur in your peripheral vision. Your awareness of where the barrel is in relation to the bird should diminish as you pull the trigger, as this is when you should see the bird the clearest.

So work on looking—*not aiming*—at the dove's beak or at the white ring on a pheasant's neck. When you learn to do this properly, you will not really see the gun but instead have a feel for where it is. You will remember seeing a part of the bird but not the bead on the gun. The bird will be clear, and the barrel will be fuzzy.

In these photos, we're using a clay target for demonstration purposes. The photo on the left indicates that you're looking at the barrel, not the bird. You want to see the bird clearly while the barrel should look fuzzy, as in the photo on the right.

The trouble is you can't get enough practice or repetition on live birds to learn to do this consistently. So you need to shoot some clay targets and practice focusing your eyes past the barrel and on the target.

At first, throw the target a few times without shooting and see if you can pick out a detail on the clay—maybe a shadow, or a glint, or the "poker chip" ring in the middle of the target. That's the equivalent of the duck's bill or the white ring on a pheasant's neck, and you need to focus on that detail. It might not sound difficult, but Anthony has spent thousands of hours learning how to keep his eye on the detail every time he fires a shot, and he says it's still the hardest part of shooting. It's difficult to not look at the barrel. You must work at it!

GETTING THE LEAD

There's an old joke about a grouse hunter who gets lost in the woods. He hasn't seen anyone for hours, but suddenly, a grouse flushes and sails across a clearing—the easiest shot imaginable. Two shots later, the bird is still flying and the hunter is shaking his head. "Where was I on that bird?" he asks. Another hunter steps out of the brush and says, "Behind it."

The answer is not always that simple, nor is "behind it" always the right answer. To shoot a moving target, you must get the muzzle of the gun some distance ahead of that target. Now, some instructors say there's no such thing as lead—if you swing the gun fast and shoot right at the bird, it will fall. We don't agree. Lead surely does exist, and if you're shooting properly, you are aware of it, even if you don't consciously think about it.

To begin with, there are three variables that determine the lead required to hit a moving target, whether it's clay or feathered: angle, speed, and distance.

Shots with little or no angle, such as decoying ducks or upland birds flying straight away, are generally easy for most hunters, as there is little lead. In fact, Will used to get away with aiming on these shots, even though it wasn't the best way to go about it. You might even think you're doing well—until you're faced with a crossing shot.

As Will demonstrated on his fateful gadwall hunt, crossing shots change things drastically, and as we add speed and distance, the shots get harder. You're going to have to put some daylight or space between the bird and muzzle to hit the shots—and as you add distance and speed, you need more daylight.

Most people try to measure this lead, and they struggle. The key is to lock your eyes on the target and see the lead only in your peripheral vision. Your brain will learn different lead pictures, but you must not measure this space in terms of feet or inches. We want you to learn a *relative* position, not an exact measure of lead.

Try to establish lead as you mount the gun. The muzzle should meet the front edge of the target or bird, such as the beak or perhaps—say, on a decoying, dropping mallard—the feet. If the bird or target is particularly far or fast, you can mount the gun a little farther in front. In other words, as you shoulder the gun, you may need to establish daylight in front of the bird through the process of mounting.

Once you mount the gun, try to match the speed of the gun with the bird. Then start focusing on the bird or target as your gun pulls away to establish the final lead. As the gun pulls away, it should move just slightly faster than the bird—if it's flying 20 miles per hour, you move at 21 to 22 miles per hour. If your eyes are locked on the bird or target, your brain will figure out the proper lead. This takes practice, but you should start to get a better understanding that lead is more of a "feel," not a measurement.

The easiest way to imagine and understand this is to compare it to throwing a football to a friend. You don't do anything except look at your buddy, and your brain tells your arm and hands where and how hard to throw the ball. You don't even think about it. Shooting a shotgun properly works the same way.

Once it all starts to come together, you'll be amazed that you don't really see the gun clearly, and that you see the lead in your peripheral vision without really looking for it. The feeling will be similar to throwing a football to a sprinting receiver. Once you learn to see the bird clearly at the end of the shot, your eyes will help your hands do the rest.

With time, you'll learn there basically are four types of leads: no lead, a little lead, medium lead, and a lot of lead. Regardless, you need to learn to see it peripherally and let your eyes finish the shot. You will build a memory bank of shots as you practice and gain experience.

These ideas may be drastically different from what you've done all your life, perhaps even different from what you've been taught. You'll have to work at it, and that will require some trips to the gun club or practice range. But if you adopt these principles, and learn how to properly look at the target, mount the gun, and generate lead, you will become a better hunter.

TYPES OF LEAD

She's on point! Your dog's tail is sticking straight up in the air and trembling just a bit—and so are you. You shuffle forward, your heart pounding and your nerves throbbing. The quail get up with a buzzing, whirring roar, and you slam your shotgun into your shoulder and look for a bird. You pick out one, stab the air in front of it, and pull the trigger.

The bird keeps on flying, and your dog gives you the evil eye before you send her on. Your partner, meanwhile, seemed to move like cold molasses, but his dog has already brought back one bird and is heading out for the second.

A few weeks later, your buddy has a flock of teal working your spread. He's kak-kak-kaking at them, and they're circling, getting ready to pitch in. They lock up and raise a wing, and suddenly, a dozen bluewings are just hanging there, 20 yards away.

You jump up and point right at one. Miss. You see another one that seems to be flying straight away and put the shotgun's bead on its butt. How'd you miss that one? And finally, you fling a prayer at a teal that hung around a hair too long and break its wing tip. Luckily, your buddy has an excellent Labrador, and the bird is soon in hand.

What happened? You got too excited and, instead of making a solid mount and move toward the bird, you just stabbed at it, hoping your shot cloud would collide with it somewhere out there. Your partner, meanwhile, took his time and pointed his gun properly, generating lead by keeping his eye on the target.

You might never get over the thrill of a covey rise or a chance to double on ducks. In fact, we hope you never really do, as that's one of the best parts about hunting. But you can learn how to consistently get your gun in the right place to make successful shots, a process we call "generating lead."

There are three basic ways to get your gun out in front of a flying bird. The basic differences are where the gun starts in relation to the bird and the speed at which you move the gun.

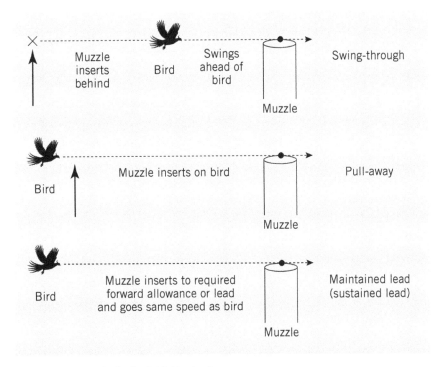

The three main methods of establishing lead.

- In **swing-through**, the gun starts behind the bird and you move a bit faster than the target, firing as the gun passes the bird.
- In **pull-away**, you place the gun on or just in front of the bird, match its speed for a moment, and then ease away from it, firing as your eyes focus in on a detail such as the bird's beak or the ring on the pheasant's neck.
- In **maintained lead**, you place the gun the proper distance in front of the bird and move with it as your eyes lock in and deliver the shot.

If you ask hunters which method they use most, they're likely to say swing-through. It's excellent for upland hunting, where many shots are quartering away or crossing at relatively close distances, and it works on decoying waterfowl and early-season doves as well. As distances grow longer, such as with late-season doves or passing shots on geese, pull-away and maintained lead may be more useful.

Whatever method you choose, you need to make sure you move your gun in sync with the bird. Many hunters think swing-through requires fast gun movement. It doesn't—you just need to move your gun a little bit faster than the bird. The same goes for pull-away. And when shooting maintained lead, your goal is to move at the same speed as the bird.

If you do this, the bird will seem to slow down and you'll see it better, greatly increasing your chances of a clean, killing shot. It's like merging into traffic from an on-ramp: if you're traveling slower than the other cars, they seem to be moving fast, and if you're moving faster than them, you need pinpoint timing to merge without causing a wreck. But if you match the speed of the other cars, they seem like they're standing still, and you can gently accelerate and pull ahead.

That's the way we want you to shoot. Ideally, you'll have a sense of *controlling* the bird, and the shot will seem easy. It works like this:

- As you mount the gun, you're looking at the bird you plan to shoot. You bring the gun up to your face and end up with the barrel pointing at the bird's head, or maybe just behind it.
- You move with it, concentrating on the bird's beak or head. As you do so, you gently accelerate, moving the gun away from the bird. If the bird's flying at 30 miles per hour, you should move at 31 or 32 miles per hour.
- As the bird comes into focus and you see a detail on it, fire!

That's swing-through and pull-away. Maintained lead works much the same, except you start the gun in front of the bird and keep it there as you swing. Knowing just where you should put the gun requires practice and experience.

With practice, generating leads becomes automatic. This may not be the case in the beginning, but in time you should be able to look at the bird, keep your eye on it, and gently accelerate to the desired lead. Over time, the goal is to allow your subconscious to generate the lead.

There's one more common upland shot: the bird that flushes straight away from you. This may appear to be the easiest shot of all,

TYPES OF SHOTGUNS

Unlike rifles, which fire a single projectile toward a target, shotguns usually fire cartridges filled with multiple metal pellets that spread during flight, making it easier to hit a moving target.

These pellets are called **shot**, and come in various metals and sizes. Lead is most often used for upland hunting and target shooting. Nonlead pellets made from other metals and alloys, such as steel, bismuth, and tungsten, are required to hunt migratory birds.

Shotguns and shotgun ammunition are classified by **gauge**, a measure of the barrel's internal size. The largest gauge is 10, while 12 is the most common and most versatile. Smaller gauges are the 16, 20, 28, and .410 caliber.

Most hunting scenarios require a gun that can shoot twice without reloading. This can be a **semiautomatic** or **autoloader**, which fires and reloads with every pull of the trigger; a **pump**, which requires the shooter to reload by manipulating the action; or a **double-barrel**, which has separate barrels that fire one after the other.

The most common double-barrel shotgun is the **over/under**, which stacks the barrels on top of each other. **Side-by-side** double-barrels—Will's favorites—are popular with bird hunters and people who love their traditional looks.

but it's also very easy to miss. First, a going-away bird gives you a very small profile to point at—usually the diameter of a soda can or even smaller. Second, few "straightaways" are flying straight. Some are angling away slightly, just enough to make you miss if you don't notice it, and most are climbing at an angle as they fly away. If you shoot right at the bird, there's a good chance you'll miss underneath.

We offer two solutions: Either shoot a gun that throws the pattern slightly high, or blot out the bird as you fire. It will feel as if you're shooting slightly too high on the bird, but by the time the shot arrives, the bird's head and neck will be in the center of your pattern.

WATCH IT

Regardless of the technique you use, you must understand that properly using your vision is equally important, and probably even more so. You must learn to be as focused as possible on a detail of the bird as you fire. Many misses are the result of not having proper focus, and that goes for experienced hunters as well as beginners. Because of that, we'll emphasize proper focus repeatedly throughout this book.

We all tend to try to aim or measure lead. Many people are taught how to aim a BB gun or .22 rifle before they try to point a shotgun. When they pick up a shotgun, they want to aim it as well. Beginning shotgun shooters often learn on an easy going-away or incoming target that can be broken by lining up the beads and pulling the trigger. That must change.

The key is keeping your eye on the target. This helps us override our natural tendency to measure the lead. If you are looking at the gun, you never will truly master the shotgun. You must rely on your hand-eye coordination to keep the gun in the right place consistently.

Remember, if we asked you to point at something, you wouldn't look at your finger—you'd look at the object. When you drive a car, you don't look at the hood—you look where you're going. To hit a baseball, you keep your eye on the ball—not the bat. Shooting a shotgun is no different. You must keep your eye on the object you want to hit, especially when it's moving. And flying birds are always moving!

All these methods have their uses, and ultimately you may want to learn them all. You won't learn them overnight. You'll need to practice on clay targets, training your hands to put the gun where it needs to be while looking only at the target. The more you repeat this process, the easier it will become and the better shot you'll be.

CHAPTER 3

EYE DOMINANCE

Some hunters squint an eye when they're shooting a shotgun, either because they need to, they've been told to, or they think it's best for them. The truth is that shotgun shooting is much easier if you keep both eyes open. Unfortunately, that's not always possible for many people. In this chapter, we'll try to teach you a bit about eye dominance and how to work through potential issues.

Most people have a dominant hand, and most also have a dominant eye. We want you to shoot a shotgun on the same side as your dominant eye, if possible. Why? Think of the dominant eye as your rear sight. When you keep your eyes on the bird, your brain will draw a line from your "shooting eye" to the muzzle to the spot where you are pointing. You shoot where you think you should be shooting.

With enough practice, most people will be able to shoot with both eyes open. Why is that a good idea? Your eyes are the data entry ports for your brain, and closing one cuts the data flow in half. Using both eyes can give you better reaction time while helping you see the target better and understand what it is doing.

Regardless, the first step is to figure out if your dominant eye is on the same side as your dominant hand.

DETERMINING DOMINANCE

The most common eye-dominance test is to punch a hole in a piece of paper, hold the paper at arm's length from your face, look through the hole at a specific object, and then close one eye. If the object is still visible through the hole, then that open eye is dominant.

That's a basic test, and it works best with people who are strongly dominant in one eye or the other. The problem with this test, or a similar one in which you look through a hole made with your hands and fingers, is that it forces you to choose the right or left eye as dominant.

It fails to account for the *degree* of dominance or what happens when a person's brain is calculating alignment with both eyes. That's because eye dominance is more of a range—someone could be 100 percent right-eye dominant, 60 percent right-eye dominant, or 90 percent left-eye dominant, or somewhere in between.

To figure out the degree of dominance, we use another test to see where your finger aligns when you're pointing at an object with both eyes open. We check the position of the index finger in correlation to your eyes, and we do this by pointing with both hands, one at a time. If both your fingers line up directly under your right eye, then we would consider you 100 percent right-eye dominant. If they are both directly under the left eye, then we would consider you 100 percent left-eye dominant. Neither is as common as many people assume.

Some people don't favor either side at all. They have what is called "center dominance." Instead of using the dominant eye to draw the line between the muzzle and the target, the brain calculates the alignment with data from both eyes. The gun points in a different position than the shooter perceives.

If your dominant eye is on the same side as your strong hand and you've been closing an eye to shoot, open it! It'll pay off. Just remember that you won't see the barrel as clearly as you did with one eye. Two-eyed shooters see the barrel as a blur—it's a reference point, not a distinct object in their vision. If you are learning to shoot with both eyes, you'll need a little time to get comfortable with looking beyond the barrel and at the target.

These photos display right, left, and center dominance.
Knowing your own dominance is crucial.

Here are some tips to help with the transition:

- Start with a basic incoming target that gives you some hang time at about 20 or 30 yards. Start with an unmounted gun, as performing the gun mount can help your hands and eyes work together as they do when you catch a ball.
- Keep your eyes on the clay. Do not try to see the lead or sight picture that you used to see when you shot with one eye closed. Work to watch the target.
- Point your index finger on your front hand along the fore-end of the gun and at the target. This helps you point more naturally and accurately.
- You can check your gun mount or alignment with one eye, but before calling "pull," make sure you open both eyes.
- Add angles and distance gradually, building on success. That helps you build your confidence as you progress to more challenging targets.

SHOOTING WITH EYE-DOMINANCE ISSUES

If your dominant hand isn't on the same side as your dominant eye— say, you're left handed but right-eye dominant—you have options.

The simplest way for a hunter who shoots clays to warm up for birds is to close the dominant eye while mounting the gun on their strong side. That makes the open eye dominant, and will fix any eye-dominance issue. While this may not be the best strategy if you want to become a champion clay shot, it might help you hit more targets.

You may see people on the clays course with a small dot or patch on their glasses, which they use to blur the vision of their dominant eye. This allows them to shoot from their strong shoulder with both eyes open. It works for clays but is a bad—and potentially dangerous— idea for hunters. You don't want to do anything to restrict your vision in the field. Squint your dominant eye instead.

A person whose "off eye" is 100 percent dominant also could consider switching shoulders. This is probably easiest for beginners or younger shooters, but with determination and hard work, even experienced shooters can do it. If you don't put in the work, however, it will feel uncomfortable and probably won't work. It may be the best long-term option, but it takes commitment and constant practice of the gun mount.

CHAPTER 4

GUN MOUNT

You may have seen clay shooters call for a target with their gun already in their shoulder. That's the way trap and skeet are usually shot in the United States, and many sporting clays shooters shoot that way as well. But as a hunter, you must start with the gun out of your shoulder. You can't walk through a field with your gun already mounted, nor can you sit in a duck blind with your shotgun ready to go.

Therefore, learning to properly mount your gun is a prerequisite for learning to let your hands and eyes work together. It helps you sync up with a target—think of the gun mount as the way you merge your gun and the bird, like merging your car in traffic.

A proper mount puts the gun under your cheekbone beneath your shooting eye. Your head should be forward on the stock, no farther than two inches from your trigger hand. The recoil pad should be in the pocket of your shoulder. If you do this properly, your shooting eye will be in line with the muzzle and the gun will go wherever your eyes go. Many people look at the gun barrel because they are trying to determine whether their eye is lined up with the muzzle. If you mount properly and practice your mount at home and on the range, there's no need to do that.

Both of your hands should move together as you bring the gun to your face—otherwise, your muzzle will dip off the target's flight line. Practice bringing the gun up to your cheek and into your shoulder so your head is down and your shooting eye is in line with the bead or beads. If your gun has two beads, the beads should touch to make a figure eight. But the beads are there only to help you mount the gun consistently. Once you get confident in your ability to mount the gun properly, you won't need to look at the beads during the shot. Frankly, you shouldn't.

A good gun mount makes shooting easier—you're comfortable, balanced, and your shooting eye is well aligned with the barrel.

Practice with your *unloaded* gun while looking in a mirror. If you've done it right, your eyes will be level and the gun will be neither so high that the recoil pad is above your shoulder nor so low that you must push down your head to get your cheek on the gun. Your shooting or master eye should be right above the rib. That turns your master eye into the equivalent of a rear sight, looking over the barrel at the target.

You can also put a dot or a piece of tape on the wall, look at the dot and practice mounting to that point, making sure both hands are moving in sync. Some people even stick a small flashlight in their muzzle and practice their mounts in a darkened room. It makes it easy to determine whether you're mounting smoothly and in line with the target by watching the movement of the flashlight's beam.

It's also a good idea to practice in your hunting clothes. There's a big difference in mounting a gun when you're wearing a thin shirt or blouse and when you're bundled up for a January goose hunt!

After a bit of practice, you'll find that you can mount the gun without thinking about it and know your eye is lined up with the muzzle every time. Then when you get into the field or on the clay range, you can mount the gun without looking back at the barrel/muzzle to check your gun mount. This will make it much easier to keep your eye on the target.

You can do all this at home, but at some point, you'll need to try it with live ammunition. That's when you go to a clays course or trap or skeet field. And even though you'll see lots of people shooting with the gun fully mounted, you should start with the gun out of your shoulder, holding it as you would when you're expecting a flush or getting ready to shoot a dove. It'll pay off in the fall.

STANCE, FORM, AND GRIP

Your stance, form, and grip allow you to move the shotgun with control, which is important for success and consistency. Think of the way a shortstop, tennis player, or boxer stands—balanced and able to move from side to side. You need that kind of balance because swinging a shotgun starts in your lower body, not your arms. A proper swing involves the rotation of your entire body, not just the arms and upper body.

You want your feet roughly shoulder width apart, with your weight slightly forward and your center of gravity under your chin. Your front knee should be bent slightly, and your weight distribution should be about 50/50 or 60/40, favoring the front foot.

Experienced shooters tend to lean forward, and novices tend to lean back. A slight forward lean isn't the end of the world, but make sure you don't wind up off balance. Try to keep your center of gravity between your feet and under your chin. That creates balance and helps you rotate.

Once you've set up with good balance and your feet are roughly shoulder width apart, you should point your leading foot toward where you think you'll shoot the bird. If you're a right-handed shooter, that's your left foot and, of course, the opposite if you're left handed. If you're set up correctly, you should be able to draw a line from your back heel through your front big toe to the spot where you're shooting. If you're caught off guard, which can happen a lot in hunting, take a small step with your leading foot toward the bird—that should get you in proper position.

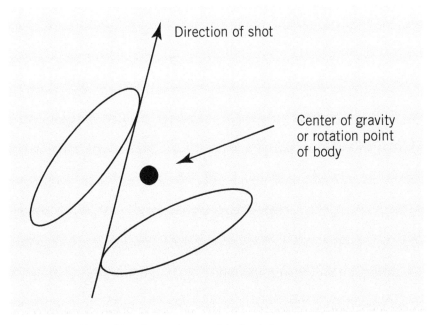

Direction of shot

Center of gravity or rotation point of body

Your feet should be positioned properly as you take the shot.
Left-handers should put their right foot forward.

Many people push off their back foot and wind up almost on tiptoe as they finish the shot. That puts them off balance and, often, out of position for a follow-up shot. They've also lost the ability to move the gun starting from the lower body, so they wind up lunging and poking at the second bird. Keep both feet firmly on the ground, and rotate around your center of gravity.

Grip: Most people don't put much thought into the grip, but it's important. You want your whole upper body to be loose, including your hands. Both hands should have about the same grip tension as you would use to handle a cracked egg, tight enough so you don't drop it but loosely enough that you don't crack it further. Most hunters grip the gun entirely too tight.

You can point your index finger toward the clay, open the palm of your hand, and let the gun sit there. Hold the fore-end where it feels comfortable—we recommend a hand position that allows for a bent elbow; this is particularly important to keep your gun from hanging up while wearing heavy clothes. Your trigger hand should be around the grip, with the pad of your forefinger or the first joint of your trigger finger resting on the trigger.

The first joint of your index finger should rest on the trigger.

HINTS

Here are a few hints to improve your gun mount:

- **Hold the gun loosely.** This allows you to move with the bird as it flushes from cover or drops to your decoys. Too tight, and you'll stiffen up.
- Some people recommend starting with the gunstock tucked under the armpit. We'd recommend that you **hold the gunstock directly under your shoulder pocket**. That way, you only need to slide the gun up to your face, instead of moving it out and then up.
- Though the front hand can start the mount, you must **move both hands together to complete the mount**. Too much movement with the back hand will make your muzzle dip.
- If you struggle, **check your head position, balance, and stance**.
- Shooters who struggle to keep their eyes level when the gun is mounted should **make sure the top of the stock is under the cheekbone**. And **turn your nose inward**, so it's close to the side of the stock.

Proper form involves balance and flexibility, allowing you to swing in different directions.

GUN FIT FOR HUNTERS

There's a lot of information out there about gun fit, and most of it is aimed at competitive clay shooters or other people trying to reach the highest level of proficiency. For hunters, it's less important to get every detail of their gun fit right, so long as they can mount the gun properly with their master eye looking down the barrel and the gun is comfortable to shoot. If the fit is so far off that you get smacked in the face or pounded in the shoulder every time you pull the trigger, then you need to make some adjustments.

In practical terms, the length of the stock—referred to as the length of pull—is very important. Most guns are designed for the average man, who stands around five feet, nine inches, and have stocks around 14½ to 14¾ inches long. That length should also work in the field for someone who is taller, perhaps with a slightly longer recoil pad. A very rough way to estimate your correct length of pull is to put the gun in the crease of your bent elbow. If your finger can easily reach the trigger, the length of pull is probably close enough. If you can't reach the trigger, the length of pull is probably too long.

If you must choose between a gun that is too long or too short, err on the side of too short—it will be easier to mount, especially if you're bundled up for cold weather. In competition, Anthony shoots a stock custom built to fit his six-foot-three frame, with a length well over 15 inches. While hunting, he generally uses a gun as it came out of the box, with no modifications.

If you're shorter or are buying a gun for a female or youth shooter, you may need to find a youth or compact stock or trim the stock a bit depending on their height. Be aware that synthetic or plastic stocks can be hard to cut, so that may weigh in to your buying decisions. A good gun-smith is your friend in this case—and save the cutoff piece of stock, as you may be able to glue it back on as a youth shooter grows.

Another important measurement is the height of comb or "drop" of the stock, which should be adjusted so your master eye is directly over the gun's rib. Too high and the gun will shoot high; too low and you may run into all sorts of problems, including blocking your shooting eye and preventing you from seeing the bird. Fortunately, many semi-automatic shotguns have shims or other means to adjust the comb of the stock to make it suit you—check YouTube or the owner's manual for directions.

For over/under shotguns and side-by-sides, you can build up the comb with moleskin or use aftermarket comb raisers such as those sold by Beretta. A good gunsmith can shave down the stock if it's too high.

Practice can help you get away with a gun that doesn't fit you perfectly. If it's a little long, slide your hand back a bit on the fore-end. If it's too low, learn how to mount it with soft cheek pressure. The challenge is to learn how to get your shooting eye in the right place with a stock that's "good enough" for the field.

If the stock length is OK and the comb height allows you to stack the barrel beads in a figure eight, you're probably in good shape. If the gun kicks you too hard, you may need to experiment with pitch, the angle that determines the way the gun fits into your shoulder. One way to do that is to slide some washers onto the butt plate screws. Put two or three on the bottom screw, retighten it, and see how that feels. Then reverse it, putting the washers on the top screw. You'll soon be on the right track.

What about a custom gun fit? If you have the money to spend, go for it. Just understand that a perfect fit doesn't help much if you don't have a good gun mount and proper technique. It can also be difficult to find a gun fitter, so ask at the local gun clubs for recommendations.

Summary:

- Hunters don't need their gun to fit precisely—it just needs to be "good enough."
- The most important measurement is length of pull, and slightly short is better than too long.
- Make sure the stock allows you to line up the beads, or see the front bead and a tiny bit of rib. A stock that's too high can be adjusted with shims or a rasp; a stock that's too low can be fixed with shims, moleskin, or a comb raiser.
- Pitch can affect recoil dramatically, but before making an irreversible decision to cut your stock, experiment by putting washers under the recoil pad.
- If you need help, ask at your local gun club for recommendations.

CHAPTER 5

EYES AND EARS

There's a saying: you can always tell an old shooter, but you can't tell them much. Why? Because they're hard of hearing.

Target shooters got the message long ago: Hearing protection should be worn every time you shoot a gun. Since firearm shots can be as loud as 160 decibels, you risk immediate hearing damage every time you pull the trigger. Over time, the damage builds up—just like the sunburns of youth can lead to skin cancer years later.

Hunters should worry about hearing protection, too—not just from their own guns but from other hunters' as well. A blast from a duck-blind companion's gun can damage your ears as surely as your own gun can.

The use of ear and eye protection is the classic story of the old-timer telling the young bucks what he wishes he had done. It doesn't matter until it matters, and at that point it's too late. Anthony wears ear and eye protection religiously when shooting clays but admits that he follows through with it in the field only half the time. We get it—it's easier not to worry about it, but we feel compelled to encourage you to do so.

Will has lost 50 percent of the hearing in his left ear from shooting when he was younger, when folks weren't as aware of the value of hearing protection. He's worn electronic protection on the range and in the field for forty years to protect the remaining hearing he has.

Don't take it just from us. Ask Dr. Grace Gore Sturdivant, a doctor of audiology and founder of OtoPro Technologies, a company that provides professional hearing protection services for shooters and other people who work or play in loud environments.

"Noise exposure injures the tiny hair cells in the cochlea that transmit sounds to the brain," she explains. "When those hair cells are injured, your ears ring. If the hair cells are able to recover, the ringing subsides, but the next injury is more likely to be permanent due to the sustained, cumulative damage."

So what's the best solution? There are many options, and you can find hearing protection to fit any budget. The key, Dr. Sturdivant said, is to get "a deep, completely sealed fit of the ear."

The easiest way to do that is with **foam earplugs**, which can be bought in bulk for just a few pennies. Gun clubs often give them away. Dr. Sturdivant says these plugs can be excellent, provided they are inserted properly. To do that, roll the plug into a tight cylinder, use your opposite hand to pull the top of your ear up and back, straightening your ear canal, and insert the plug. Keep your finger on it until it completely expands.

Some people can't wear foam plugs—their ear canal simply won't allow it. While Anthony uses foam plugs every day while teaching shooters, Will can't because his ear canal won't allow the foam plug to stay in place. He needs another option.

Those include **earmuffs**, either passive or with electronics that amplify quiet sounds and cut off at the sound of a gunshot. Good-quality passive muffs can be found for $30 or less, and usable electronic muffs are available for about $75.

Want the ultimate in hearing protection? Combine custom-fit earplugs with a pair of muffs.

Like everything else, earmuffs have their drawbacks. Passive muffs cut off all sound, so you might not hear a turkey's gobble or the whistling wings of ducks coming from behind. All muffs can be too hot to use in the summertime, and some people cannot mount their gun properly with muffs.

The next option is **custom-molded earplugs**—solid or filtered, or electronic, like Will wears. They require molds to be made by a competent professional; an audiologist or hearing aid specialist can do it. At the top end of the price range, these plugs can stream music or phone calls through Bluetooth technology while amplifying the sounds around you.

A good compromise for hunters is **custom-molded plugs with replaceable impulse filters**. They allow soft sounds to pass through to the eardrum unfiltered but shut off when a shot is fired. While not cheap, they are far less expensive than electronic plugs and don't require batteries or recharging. You can even buy specialized filters to wear while attending music concerts.

Just don't use AirPods or other standard earbuds that pair up with smartphones or other devices. They don't seal the ear canal, so they don't give you any protection.

HEARING AIDS

Many hunters wear hearing aids. Dr. Sturdivant recommends taking out hearing aids while hunting and shooting and using regular hearing protection instead.

Why not just turn off the hearing aids? In most cases, hearing aids leave the ear canal open, so they don't provide any protection. Electronic earplugs, however, provide more amplification of quiet sound yet still block the gun blast.

ABOUT THE EYES

Even if you don't need corrective lenses, you should strongly consider wearing protective glasses while hunting. They'll protect your eyes from thorns, weeds, brambles, and the occasional spritz of unburnt gunpowder coming out of your pump or autoloader. Even more important, pellets can sometimes ricochet off trees or rocks, and in a worst-case scenario, quality protective glasses can save your vision in the case of a hunting accident.

Clay target shooters often purchase lenses in multiple colors to enhance their vision under different conditions. But for hunters, a pair of clear or lightly tinted lenses for overcast conditions and a pair of darker tinted lenses for sunny conditions are probably enough.

Try the glasses before you wear them in the field. Some models hug the face too closely and then steam up under warm conditions. Others may be comfortable in the store but slip and slide down your nose once you start sweating.

Eyeglasses wearers usually can wear their regular glasses and prescription sunglasses. But it's worth investing in a special pair of prescription shooting lenses, available from many vendors. They're ground slightly differently so you get the best optical results while looking through the top part of the lens, as you do when you are peering over the rib of your shotgun.

What about sunglasses? They're better than nothing, but few are designed to provide protection. Spend a little more—your vision is worth it.

CHAPTER 6

UPLAND HUNTING

Upland hunting is perhaps the broadest category of wing shooting, ranging from woodcock flitting through the aspen popple to big cackling pheasants rocketing out of cattails or brushy ravines. You can hunt bobwhite quail from the back of a mule-drawn wagon easing its way through a pine forest, you can bloody your forearms trying to bull your way through ruffed grouse cover, you can trek for miles seeking

Hungarian partridge and sharp-tailed grouse on the prairies, or you can chase desert quail among the cactus and rocks of the Southwest.

Some hunters follow their setters through cover while carrying imported side-by-sides that can cost more than a new pickup, and others lug their dad's rusty pump gun as they follow their Labradors across the prairies. Some hunters seek the wildest places, miles from any road and out of cell phone range, while others take their children to preserves not far from the city to get their first taste of upland adventures.

Some upland shooting is easier than pass-shooting doves or waterfowl—but that doesn't mean it can't be a challenge. Choosing the right equipment and mastering a few basic techniques can go a long way toward filling your hunting vest with birds in the fall.

EQUIPMENT

Almost any shotgun will work in at least a few upland hunting scenarios. Pump shotguns have probably accounted for more pheasants killed in the United States than any other type of gun, and light, fast-handling semiautos or lightweight over/unders and side-by-sides are the choice of many quail hunters, particularly in the West. The traditional ruffed grouse gun is a side-by-side. The key is to have at least two shots available, and to fire a cartridge that's adequate for the bird you're hunting.

But if there's any typical scenario where a fine double is especially appropriate, it's upland hunting. Anthony favors over/under shotguns in 20 gauge or 28 gauge, while Will loves side-by-sides ranging from .410 to 16 gauge—even more so if they're old-fangled hammer guns. These nicer guns won't get banged up like a waterfowl gun even if they're hunting ruffed grouse in thick woods or Mearns quail in the Arizona mountains, and there's a special joy in shooting beautiful birds with beautiful guns.

A day afield is one to remember, even more so if you happen to shoot well with a beautiful shotgun.

The most versatile gauge for upland hunters is the 12. You can buy light, ⅞-ounce target loads that are the equivalent to shooting a 20 gauge, or you can find shells that might be better suited for a pterodactyl than a bird. For many others the 20 gauge or the 28 gauge is a favorite. There are plenty of suitable choices, whether you're hunting pheasants, quail, grouse, or woodcock.

Many hunters find a 20-gauge shotgun adequate for all upland hunting, and they enjoy the handling qualities of a smaller, lighter gun, particularly in the grouse woods or on a fast-flushing covey rise. It might not be the best choice for long-range pheasants at the end of the season, but with proper loads, it's lethal to 40 yards even on strong-flying roosters.

The 28 gauge is more of a specialist's gun—great for small birds at close range, such as bobwhite quail and woodcock. Some expert shots with good pointing dogs use it for pheasants, but you must be careful about shot selection and be willing to pass up any borderline shots.

On a shooting preserve, where the shots tend to be closer, a 28 gauge is excellent.

We're not huge fans of the .410 caliber for hunting except for expert shots with a keen awareness of their own abilities. Even for them, a 28 gauge is likely to be a more effective choice.

A quick word about the 16: Many hunters consider it the greatest upland gauge of all, a hard-hitting but light-carrying gun that isn't over-kill for smaller birds and is more than adequate for the big ones. The trouble is that 16-gauge guns can be hard to find, and 16-gauge ammo scarcer yet. Some 16s are built on 12-gauge frames, which means they weigh just about as much as a 12 in the same model. That wipes out the main reason for having one. But if you own or find a light 16 that pleases you and you plan to purchase adequate supplies of shells, a 16 can be an absolute dream in the field.

Regardless of the gauge you choose, you should pay attention to weight. Upland guns are carried a lot and shot relatively little, except perhaps in good quail country. For that reason, hunters tend to look for lighter guns, sometimes less than six pounds and with barrels as short as 24 or 26 inches. But be careful: A gun that is too light and too short is hard to control, and there's not much point in carrying a gun for miles if you can't shoot it well!

We think the sweet spot for upland guns for most hunters is between six and seven and a half pounds. That gives you enough mass to swing the gun smoothly, and it's not too much to carry for a few hours. As for barrel length, we recommend 28 to 30 inches for doubles and 26 to 28 inches for pumps and semiautos. That's long enough for a good sighting plane and not so heavy that you can't carry it.

Shorter barrels can be an advantage in thick cover, though, and if you've got a gun that weighs less than six pounds and you can shoot well, have at it—just don't try to shoot heavy loads through it. Even one magnum shell through a light gun can be an experience you won't want to repeat. Some of us are bigger and tougher than others, so choose your payload accordingly.

What about shells? For most upland birds, ⅞ ounces to 1⅛ ounces of shot works well depending on gauge. For quail and woodcock, No. 8 and No. 7½ lead shot are good, and for ruffed grouse or prairie grouse, use No. 7½ or go up to No. 6. Three-inch shells are almost never necessary.

Pheasants are a different story, as they can present longer shots in open cover. For those birds, you probably want a minimum of an ounce of No. 6 shot. And 1¼ ounces of No. 5 or No. 4 lead shot may even be better, particularly in the late season, over flushing dogs, or if you have no dog at all. A wounded pheasant can run faster than most hunters, and if you don't anchor it with an adequate shot load, your odds of recovering the bird drop significantly.

If you want a single do-it-all load, think about an ounce to 1¼ ounces of No. 6 shot. That should work on almost every bird if you keep your shots within reasonable range—say, 40 yards or less.

Some areas require nontoxic shot, and steel is the most commonly available option—but it's best used in the 12 gauge and perhaps the 20. No. 6 shot is good for smaller birds, but go up to No. 3, 4, or 5 for pheasants or prairie grouse. Again, you want a minimum load of 1 ounce.

The emergence of bismuth and tungsten shot has made smaller gauges more practical in nontoxic scenarios, and since you don't typically shoot much on an upland hunt, the additional cost of these premium loads isn't unbearable. Their extra downrange energy can allow you to take somewhat longer shots in some scenarios.

Improved cylinder is probably the best all-around choke, regardless of gauge, though pheasant hunters often choose modified if they're hunting with a flushing dog or "pushing" birds with a big group of friends. In a double, it's a good idea to have different chokes, depending on your quarry. Skeet and improved cylinder would work well for grouse and bobwhite hunters under most conditions; light modified and improved modified isn't out of place on the prairies. For an all-around pairing, improved cylinder and modified are as good as anything.

FIELDCRAFT

There's not much more nerve-rattling than a rooster pheasant blowing up out of the snow at your feet, unless it's a dozen quail erupting at the same time, buzzing in different directions like popcorn. Those moments get your heart pounding, and for many of us, they make us love upland hunting . . . and they drive us up a wall. We've all been there: the bird rockets up, you slam your gun to your shoulder, and two or three shots later, the bird is still flying away.

The truth is that most shots in the uplands are relatively easy, at least compared to pass-shooting doves or geese. Those explosive flushes make them difficult. They get our adrenaline pumping, and we move way too fast, often emptying the gun while the bird is still in easy shooting range. Some people call those moments the "bang-bang-darns"—or something a bit saltier.

How can you get past that? Experience surely helps. A bobwhite covey flush won't seem so chaotic after you've seen a hundred of them.

You also can learn how to read a dog. Most hunters know that when a dog's on point, there's usually a game bird close by. Then it's a matter of walking briskly to the dog and moving in from the side or front. (*Don't* walk directly behind a pointing dog. Let the dog see you—that will keep it calmer and steadier.)

Walk in on a point confidently and ready to shoot!

But what about a flusher? Can you tell when a springer's about to roust a pheasant out of a cattail slough, or a cocker is about to find a grouse in the thicket? Surely having a dog of your own can help there. But if you don't, pay attention to your friends and guides as they handle a dog. Ask them what to look for as their dog is seeking out game. Being as prepared for a flush as possible is half the battle.

Don't try to spot the birds on the ground. They're usually well camouflaged. Instead, walk in on the point or walk behind the dog with your eyes gazing off into the distance, in the direction you expect the bird to flush. That helps you pick up the bird in your peripheral vision as it gets off the ground. Then start looking for a detail on the bird, something to focus on as you mount your gun and take the shot. The classic is the white band that gives the ringneck pheasant his name, but you also can be looking at the bird's eye or beak. Some proficient bobwhite quail hunters can even distinguish the hen's rusty face markings from the male's snowy mask.

Then when the bird gets up, *slow down*! The biggest mistake most hunters make is shooting too quickly, fearing that the birds are getting out of range. Do the math: a pheasant at top speed may be going 50 miles per hour with a tailwind, but he's not flying that fast right away. Meantime, your shotgun pellets are traveling at 800 miles per hour or better. Guess who's going to win that race?

Besides, if you center a bird at 10 yards or so, there's not going to be much left for dinner. The ideal gunning distance in the uplands is between 20 and 35 yards. Forty yards is a long shot, and most people should pass it up, especially if they're not confident in their capabilities.

You should be walking with the gun near armpit level. As the bird gets up, take a step toward it with your leading foot (left foot for right handers, right foot for lefties) as you slowly bring your gun to your face. Most shots will be either straightaways or at quartering angles, with very little lead needed. Point your gun at the bird and move with it, and when you see the detail on the bird clearly, pull the trigger. Then wait for the dog to bring back your prize.

You need to practice holding the gun and mounting it correctly even when surprised. The pictures with this chapter illustrate ways to carry the gun safely, assuming that you are always pointing the muzzle in a safe direction. Practice at home with an unloaded gun and on the clays course to ensure a good gun mount in the field.

Always make sure your gun is pointed in a safe direction while in the uplands.

Ultimately, it's better to be smooth than fast, and it's easier to be smooth if you move relatively slowly. Just don't be surprised if that slow, steady gun mount helps you shoot faster and more accurately than you did when you were slamming your gun to your shoulder and blazing away. Review our gun mount chapter as you prepare for upland season.

You'll pick up other bits of fieldcraft and knowledge with time. For example, a quail is unlikely to fly out of cover into the open. Ruffed grouse often head for thicker cover, too. Pheasants would rather run than fly, so it's often a good idea to send a friend ahead to block their escape route. Try to learn something new on every hunt. After all, everyone was a beginner once, and even now, after decades of experience, we learn something every time out. Animals are creatures of habit—learn how they behave.

SAFETY

One of the most important concepts of safe upland shooting is to know where your hunting partners are at any moment. Especially in dense cover, it's easy for someone to drag behind or forge ahead of the rest of the group—and into the line of fire if a bird flushes unexpectedly. Blaze orange, required by many states, is a good idea even when it isn't mandatory. So is eye protection, as pellets can ricochet off trees and back at you. If you ever get a thorn or a foxtail in your eye, you'll remember your shooting glasses the next time.

Never take the safety off your gun until you're mounting it to take a safe shot at a bird. Hunters who take off the safety as they're walking in on a point or following a flusher are asking for trouble. A fall at the wrong time could imperil the dog or other hunters. Make sure, too, that the safety is back on after you've shot. It isn't a bad idea to keep checking it during the hunt. Again, you should practice taking off the safety as you mount, using an unloaded gun at first. Later, you can combine it with actual shooting on the clays course.

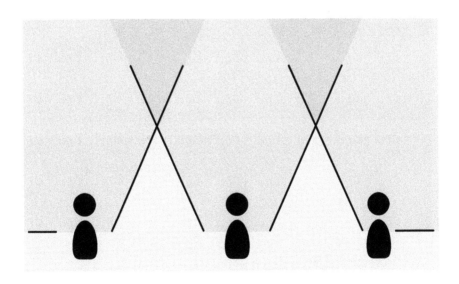

Maintain safe zones of fire when you're moving through an upland field, and don't swing too far to the left or right.

Here's how you should turn if a bird flushes and flies behind you—keep your muzzle pointed up at all times.

Avoid low shots. Too many dogs are injured each year by hunters shooting at low-flying birds—and at times, other hunters are hit as well. A good rule of thumb is to not shoot unless you see sky under the bird or you are certain of what is beyond your target. If that's impossible—such as when you're hunting in the grouse woods—make sure the bird is higher than the brim of your cap. Ultimately you must decide whether a shot is safe. Make good decisions, and remember that you can always find another bird, but a hunting accident will haunt you forever.

Flushes can rattle anyone, particularly a new hunter. Remind yourself to slow down and not bang off a shot right away. Take a second to see where the bird is going. You'll probably have better success, and more importantly, you will know that you are shooting in a safe direction.

If a bird flushes behind you or flies back over you, make sure you turn around with the gun pointed in the air. Keeping it in your shoulder pocket may sweep the muzzle past your hunting partner.

Above all, be willing to pass up a shot if you have even the slightest hint that there might be a problem. You can always find another bird—if not today, then tomorrow.

ETHICAL SHOOTING

Not all shots in the uplands are created equal, and understanding this is key to being an ethical upland hunter.

It's one thing to shoot a double on pheasants in a picked cornfield, where the birds will be easily recovered. Take the exact same shots in a dense cattail marsh, and you'll be hard-pressed to find both birds without an excellent retriever. An ethical hunter knows the difference.

Similarly, it's one thing to shoot a crossing bird at 40 yards, and another thing to shoot the bird at the same distance going away. In the first scenario, the bird's head and neck are vulnerable, increasing your chances of making a clean kill. In the second, you're shooting at the bird's body from behind—a target about the size of a soda can on end—and you must drive the pellets through the bird's rear and guts to reach the vitals. If you don't break a wing or leg, chances are good that bird will wind up in a coyote's stomach.

If you don't have a dog, consider getting one. Many hunters wouldn't even consider going out without a well-trained dog, which not only can recover birds but can help you make easier shots at closer range.

Hunters in groups should determine their personal zones of fire and take care not to shoot birds that are presenting a better shot to another hunter. Doing that can get you a reputation as a game hog, and game hogs don't get many invitations to go hunting.

Know your capabilities, and know the capabilities of your gun and cartridge. Can you kill a pheasant outright at 40 yards with No. 8 shot from a 28 gauge? Probably, but a crippling shot is far more likely. Anglers often use lighter tackle to increase their enjoyment, but there's nothing enjoyable about crippling a bird that isn't recovered. Fish that break a light line swim off to be caught another day, but a grouse or quail peppered with shot will suffer before dying, either in the jaws of a predator or bleeding out slowly.

When in doubt, don't shoot.

PRACTICING

A trap range is perhaps the best possible site to practice for upland hunting, particularly if you can get permission to shoot at distances closer than the regulation 16-yard line. Trap targets are thrown at different, unpredictable angles, so they will do a good job of replicating a going-away or quartering shot by an upland bird. Those are by far the most common shots in upland hunting, though sometimes you do get crossing shots.

For crossing shots, you can get excellent practice on stations 3, 4, and 5 on the skeet field. Skeet was invented by grouse hunters in the American Northeast, and it still offers a wide variety of shots that you'll have to replicate in the field.

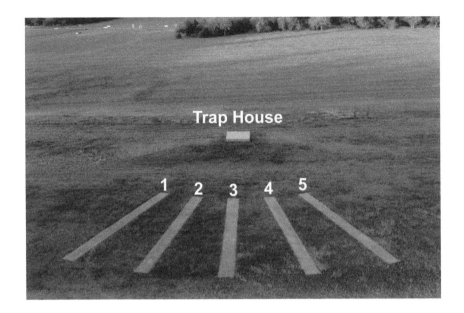

In trap, the targets are always flying away from you, though the angles may vary.

Skeet is an American game, but the layout is the same all over the world.

Sporting clays offers a blend of both, and if you want to skip the stations that don't present realistic hunting presentations, feel free to do so. Look for stations that offer quartering birds and other outgoers at reasonable distances, and some in the woods.

In any case, you should start with the gun out of your shoulder, even though you'll see dedicated clay target shooters starting with a mounted gun. That's undoubtedly the best way to score well on some targets, but our purpose is to be better shots in the field—and you never walk through the field with the safety off and the gun already at your shoulder (or at least you shouldn't!).

On the trap field, stand with your feet about shoulder width apart and your weight evenly balanced between them. Your gun should be about at the level of your armpit, or where you would be holding it as you walked behind a dog in anticipation of a flush. Your eyes should be gazing off into the distance above the trap, just as you would if you were expecting a bird to appear.

When you call "pull," the clay will pop out, flying away from you. Don't panic! The target's flying just over 40 miles per hour, and the pellets from your shotgun are far faster. It's not getting away, so don't rush. Besides, in the field you will need to learn how to take an extra heartbeat or two to make sure that your shot is safe and you're firing at a legal game bird. It's easy to get excited and accidentally shoot a wild hen pheasant, for instance. Take your time and make sure.

As the target flies, take a small step with your leading foot (remember, left foot for right handers, right foot for lefties) toward the target. That should get your feet in proper position. As you do that, bring the gun up smoothly to your face, as we described in the chapter on gun mount. As it reaches your cheek, you should see the target as clearly as possible, focusing on a detail like the rings on top or the black edge. Once you see that clearly, fire!

Because the angles usually aren't very wide, you can do very well by just looking at the bird and shooting. At longer distances or at wider angles, you may need to use one of the methods of generating lead that we discussed earlier. For most upland shooting, that will probably be a swing-through shot. In this, you would bring the gun up to your face while moving to the bird. Ideally, you'll complete the mount and

USING YOUR EYES AND THE "STEP" FOR UPLAND

If you hunt a fair amount behind a dog, you'll learn to recognize when the dog is about to flush or point a bird. At that moment, many hunters' inclination is to try to spot the rooster or covey on the ground, and that's exactly the wrong thing to do. Instead, we want you to feel as if you're gazing toward the horizon, what we call "soft focus" in clay target shooting. The best comparison to this is zooming out on a camera lens, taking in as much of the landscape as possible.

When you're in soft focus, it's much easier to pick up movement. That means that when the bird flushes, you will pick it up quickly—and that's when you start zooming back in, just like you zoom in with your camera. At the same time, you step toward the bird (again, left foot if you're right handed, right foot if you're left handed) and start moving your hands to begin your gun mount. When you see a detail of the bird clearly, such as a rooster pheasant's white neck ring or red eye patch, you fire.

Remember, you're simply trying to pick up the flash of the bird flushing. That's the signal to step toward the bird and do everything else that follows.

The step toward the bird gives you proper foot position and greatly improves your ability to mount and swing the gun. As you walk in on the point or follow your flusher, keep gazing out into space and then zoom in on the bird with your eyes as it rises from the cover. Make sure you're not trying to see the bird too well too soon, step toward the bird, and then lock your eyes on the bird. Delayed visual acquisition and failing to step toward the bird are the most common reasons for missed shots we should typically be able to hit.

accelerate slightly, pushing the muzzle past the target and then pulling the trigger. It takes good timing and some practice, so keep at it.

Beware of trying to shoot too quickly. Your muzzle will jump all over the place, and your shots will be erratic. You'll find that the smoother you are, the faster you can fire an accurate shot. It may help to practice mounting your gun at home with a mini flashlight in the end of your barrel to ensure a minimal amount of muzzle movement.

If you want to practice shooting doubles, ask the club manager if you can shoot chips from your broken targets. This can be great fun and helpful in learning how to make a quick follow-up shot. But if the manager says no, don't push it. In the same vein, you can ask if you can shoot twice at each target, but some clubs won't allow it as it is against the rules of American trap and skeet.

You can set up a similar practice layout using your own clay target thrower. The trap probably won't throw at different angles, so take shots from various positions behind it. Just make sure that the person throwing the clays for you is always in a safe location.

CHAPTER 7

DOVES

The mourning dove is one of the most popular game birds in the United States, with hundreds of thousands of hunters shooting millions of them each year. It's also one of the most challenging—a swift and swerving gray streak that ties shooters in knots and leaves them shaking their heads in frustration.

Why are they so popular? Plenty of reasons. There are 150 million or more doves in the United States, and they can be hunted in all but a handful of the 48 continental states. They're some of the best wild food you will ever taste. The season usually opens before any other season, and with generous bag limits, you get a lot of shooting.

How much? By some estimates, the average hunter shoots seven shells to kill one dove. That's a lot! If the estimate is correct, then hunters fired more than 60 million shells at doves in 2022 and killed about 9 million of them, according to harvest figures from the U.S. Fish & Wildlife Service. With dove limits usually averaging around a dozen birds, average hunters would need more than three boxes of shells to fill a daily limit.

If you only hunt doves on opening day, this may seem a bit odd. Early-season doves eagerly fly toward decoys, either spinning-wing models or stationary ones clipped in the branches of a bare tree. The waves of doves that greet early-season hunters also let you pick your shots, greatly improving your success. Similarly, shooting doves at a watering spot in the afternoon can offer easy incoming shots and quick limits. Even so, there are always days when you run out of shells way too quickly.

Come back a few weeks later, and the game has changed. Fully feathered doves are strong and fast, and they warily skirt brush lines and other bits of cover where hunters might hide. Fall winds make them even faster, and shots are harder to come by. Even a very good shooter should be happy with just a few birds in those conditions. A late-season limit is an accomplishment!

Fortunately, dove practice is easy to find. Every skeet range and most sporting clays ranges offer shots that are familiar to dove hunters. With some late-summer practice using the techniques described in this chapter, you should be ready.

EQUIPMENT

It's hard to imagine a shotshell that won't kill a dove. Even the tiny .410 can be used with success by experienced shooters who are patient enough to choose their shots.

Most people will choose a 20- or a 12-gauge shotgun, with a few people favoring a 28 gauge. Side-by-sides, over/unders, pumps, and semiautos all work well, but if you believe that a 20-gauge gas-operated semiauto is the ultimate dove gun, we won't argue.

Open your chokes, especially in the early season. A 20 gauge with an improved cylinder choke is terrific for any dove within 30 or 35 yards, and few people can consistently knock down doves beyond that range. Even then, long shots often lead to lost birds, as a wounded bird can hobble away before the hunter can arrive to pick it up.

You can't go wrong with quality target ammunition with premium No. 8 or No. 7½ shot. Regardless of the gauge, you seldom need more than an ounce of shot. If you are required to shoot nontoxic shot on your dove field, No. 6 steel is the way to go. By the way, studies have shown that hunters have almost the same success rate on doves whether they're shooting steel or lead.

As always, hearing protection is a good idea. Dove hunters will hear almost as many shots in a day as clay target competitors. And even if you don't need prescription shooting glasses, wear protective lenses while dove shooting. On some fields it's almost a guarantee that you'll be sprinkled with shot—in the worst scenario, you might get peppered by an unsafe hunter across the way.

Camouflage helps, both on your head and on your body, but you can get away with dark khaki or olive green shirts. Blaze orange is *not* recommended, as doves will flare from it. You should also sit or stand still as the birds approach. If they see you move, you won't get a good shot—you might not even get a chance.

FIELDCRAFT

Take advantage of cover to hide yourself. Tuck into a row of corn, sit in the shade under a tree, even build a small blind if you can. The better hidden you are, the easier your shots will be.

Even if you're wearing camouflage, it's a good idea to hide in the available cover.

If you like using a spinning-wing decoy, set it off to one side rather than directly in front of your stand. That way, doves approaching the decoy won't see you stand up and shoot.

It's a good idea to use your decoys to mark distances or to step off distances before the shooting begins so you know whether a bird is flying within your effective range. Remember, wounding rates go up and recovery rates go down as distances increase.

Wait until the last possible moment to stand and shoot. You'll get better with experience, and the doves will be closer when you do pull the trigger.

Well-trained dogs are a huge help, but dogless hunters need a strategy for recovering their birds. When you knock down a dove, mark a line to where it fell. Then unload your gun and walk out into the field to pick it up. Waiting to pick up doves often results in lost birds. Make sure your hunting partners know you're going out to pick up a bird, and hurry back to your stand so you can reload and keep hunting.

But don't take your gun along. Why not? You rarely shoot a crippled dove, for one thing—they're easy to chase down. And more than once, a hunter carrying a loaded gun outside his stand has taken a shot at a passing dove in exactly the wrong direction. Well-managed dove fields are set up so that every stand shoots in a safe direction—you can't be sure of a safe shot if you're thirty yards away from your post.

SAFETY

As mentioned, wear eye protection! Even at 100 yards, some shotgun pellets retain enough energy to penetrate a soft eyeball.

Dove hunters should make special note of where other hunters are around them. Shooting down the line of hunters is dangerous, and a sure way to ensure that you won't be invited back to hunt with that group. If other hunters are out in front of their stands retrieving doves, be extra careful. Better yet, take a break until they're back on their stand.

Above all, *avoid low shots*! Most dove hunters insist that you see sky beneath a dove before pulling the trigger. It's a great rule.

DOUBLING UP ON DOVES

Doubling or tripling on a passing wad of doves is a memorable event for anyone. But before you even try it, make sure that you plan to pay extra attention to where the doves hit the ground after your shot. There's nothing worse than knocking down two doves and recovering neither. If you're shooting over a weedy field or other thick cover, stick to shooting singles unless you have a good dog with you.

Other than that, shooting doubles is not too much different than shooting singles. Pick out a bird and focus in on its beak or eye, pull the trigger, and watch where it falls. If the dove is hit but still flying, forget the double and shoot it again.

If you have killed the first bird cleanly, you may have time to unmount your gun, shift your gaze to pick out another bird, and do it again, smoothly mounting the gun to your face while focusing on the dove's beak or eye. Otherwise, keep the gun in your shoulder pocket but lift your head to pick out your next bird. Do your best to note where each dove falls. Even if you have a good line on it, a dove has an uncanny way of disappearing on the ground. A trained dog is a definite asset.

PRACTICING

A skeet field or sporting clays course offers great practice for doves. You get almost every type of shot imaginable—crossing and quartering shots in either direction, long incomers, and fast overhead shots.

One of the few potential drawbacks to the skeet field is that most regulation shots are taken within 25 yards. If you can get permission from the club management, spend some time shooting 5 to 10 yards behind the stations. Sporting clays offers shots at all angles and distances.

Regardless of the game you choose, you should avoid shooting regulation rounds when you're warming up for dove season. You won't get the repetition you need to get better. Instead, shoot a box or two of shells at only three or four stations, focusing on crossing shots and incoming shots.

Many clay shooters call for the target with a mounted gun, but you shouldn't. A smooth mount from a low gun is important for all hunters, and dove shooters are no different. Start with the gun just below your armpit and toward the center of your body. As the target appears, start moving your hands slowly to mount the gun, matching the target's speed as you merge with it. Use the variety of shots on a skeet field or clays course to learn how lead or forward allowance increase or decrease as the angles change.

At short distances, you want to be either right on the target's nose or a little bit in front of it when the gun reaches your face and shoulder. Accelerate a tad and pull the trigger, looking at the target as hard as possible. Then admire your break.

Ultimately you want to build confidence on shots up to about 35 yards or so, a reasonable distance for a dove shooter. To help you do that, revisit the chapter on generating lead and the methods of doing so.

TALL SHOTS

If you can find a sporting clays course with a tall tower—say, 40 to 60 feet high—you can get some of the best practice imaginable. Crossing targets off a tall tower are some of the most realistic dove shots you can find with clays. You shoot them in much the same way as you would the lower targets on a skeet field: Mount on or just in front of the bird; then match its speed before gently pulling away to establish lead.

What about an incomer? A tall dove that crumples in the sky and lands almost at your feet is a shot to remember, and with the proper technique and some practice, it should be relatively easy.

First, understand that most people overestimate the height of targets and birds. It's a very tall tree that stands more than 90 feet high, so a bird that crosses a treetop is likely less than 30 yards high. Yet every year, we see dove hunters passing up incoming birds that are no more than 25 yards above them but blazing away at birds passing 45 yards away. It doesn't make any sense!

When you see a high dove approaching, stay still. A dove will pick up any movement you make and flare away. As it gets within good range, mount just behind it and swing through, pulling the trigger as the gun passes through or accelerates past the dove. If you've taken the shot in the right spot, the bird will fall in front of your stand.

What's the right spot? Somewhere between 15 and 20 yards out in front. Avoid shooting birds directly overhead. For one thing, you may wind up off balance with a loaded gun in your hands—not the best scenario. Even if you hit the bird, it's likely to drop behind you and may be difficult to find if you don't see it fall.

If you're lucky enough to find a clays course with an incoming tower shot, you can practice this shot repeatedly. If not, the best option is shooting Low One and High Six on the skeet field.

Another common shot is a high dove coming from behind. They may surprise you, but sometimes your hunting partner will holler that they are coming behind you, or you'll catch them out of the corner of your eye, or see a shadow on the ground in front of you. The trick here is to shoot under the bird, as that is the proper way to generate lead. Visualize the flight line of where you expect the bird to be—and shoot "ahead" of it, which is under it.

Hunter

You must shoot under a high, going-away bird.

Ideally, you mount the gun just slightly under the bird and move with it for a heartbeat before pulling the trigger. Keep the gun moving, and be careful not to take a low shot! If you can't find this shot on a clays course, try station 1 high house on the skeet field.

LEARNING FROM DOVES

Dove hunting is a great way to get ready for the longer season ahead. For starters, it's one of the first opportunities—if not *the* first—to get out into the field. The weather is usually warm, making it a great time to get your whole family out with you and enjoy the day, perhaps enjoying a barbecue with your friends after the hunt.

You don't have to be perfectly quiet; you don't have to be perfectly still all the time. All you need is a stool, a camouflage shirt, some target loads, ear and eye protection, and your shotgun, as well as a place to go shooting.

It's also one of the most challenging forms of wing shooting, offering lots of different angles and presentations. Doves can help you figure out the truth about your shooting ability early enough in the season that you can go to work and be better prepared for upland birds or waterfowl later in the fall.

You won't do well in the dove fields if you don't look at the birds properly, or if you're trying to line up the beads for every shot. Your gun mount needs to be solid and consistent; you must figure out angles, distances, and speeds; and you often get plenty of chances. If you shoot a single box of 25 shells or less and walk out of the field with a limit of 12 or 15 doves, pat yourself on the back—you're ready for the rest of the season.

CHAPTER 8

WATERFOWL

You're flat on your back in a frozen cornfield as a skein of 12-pound geese glides overhead, and you're trying to keep still, even though you're so cold you're shivering. Or you're sweating in a southern coastal marsh, swatting mosquitos and waiting for a flock of tiny teal to buzz your decoys. Or you're crouched at the side of a beaver pond at first light, preparing to ambush the wood ducks' dawn patrol. If

you're lucky, you're hugging an oak tree in the Mississippi delta, your heart pounding as mallards filter through the tree limbs and flutter toward you.

Waterfowl hunting offers a wider variety of experiences than any other form of hunting, and that goes for its shooting challenges as well. To be a complete shot, you need to be competent in all the scenarios mentioned in the previous paragraph, and quite a few others. Go on a mixed-bag hunt where you might shoot diving ducks and puddle ducks from the same blind. Some shots will be easy—just point at the bird and pull the trigger. Others, like a bull canvasback crossing at top speed, can challenge anyone, and it's all in a day's hunt.

EQUIPMENT

Waterfowl hunters argue about ammunition and gun selection all the time. Do you use steel shot, or do you pay the extra money for a premium nontoxic load such as bismuth or a tungsten blend such as Hevi-Shot? Do you pick a heavy, gas-operated 12 gauge to soak up the recoil from stout magnum shells, or do you grab a light, fast-handling 20 gauge to tackle teal? We haven't even begun to discuss the merits of a pump shotgun, or the never-ending arguments about what size shot is best and whether there is an all-around load that can handle everything from teal to giant Canada geese.

We believe that the key is to pick the gun and shell that is most appropriate to the birds you're chasing. An early-season wood duck hunt over a pond calls out for a lighter load—say, a 2¾-inch or 3-inch 12-gauge cartridge with an ounce or 1⅛ ounces No. 4 or No. 6 steel shot. Will, who spends a lot of time in the flooded timber of the South, chooses a 20 gauge with No. 4 steel shot, as most of his shots are 30 yards or less. Under other conditions, such as a late-season river hunt in high winds for mallards and black ducks, you need a bigger shell. In Anthony's case, he reaches for a 3-inch or 3½-inch Winchester shell loaded with No. 1 or No. 2 steel shot.

Why steel? Anthony says he has no problem killing his ducks and geese with steel, but he's aware of its limitations. Even though he can break clay targets consistently at 60 yards or more, Anthony tries to limit his shots to 45 yards with steel and, when necessary, he turns to bigger pellets and a tighter choke, such as modified. At other times, he'll turn to Winchester bismuth shells for even better long-range performance.

Steel tends to pattern tighter than lead, but it's a good idea to shoot a few patterns at your usual ranges, to see which load your gun and choke combination handles best.

Many people, particularly those who like to shoot smaller-gauge shotguns, may well benefit from tungsten blends or bismuth, but they will pay a higher price for that performance. Will is one of those, frequently choosing a 20-gauge shell designed for use in vintage guns. He doesn't use a 12 gauge for ducks.

Anthony prefers a gas-operated semiauto over an inertia-operated gun, largely because of the recoil reduction of the gas gun. He also thinks that semiautos point very well—he shot one for the first twenty years of his competitive career, winning the national championship in sporting clays and two U.S. Opens along the way. But neither he nor Will sees anything wrong with a pump gun, provided you can take the recoil. Will shoots some ducks with his pet side-by-sides, and other than a fast third shot to anchor a cripple, he isn't giving up much.

In the early season, when puddle ducks decoy better and teal and wood ducks might show up, consider an improved cylinder choke. The ducks don't have the feather padding they will have later in the year, nor will they have as much fat. If little ducks are ripping through your decoys at 20 or 30 yards, you want to open your pattern. A 25-yard teal centered with a modified choke doesn't leave much for the table. Nor does the modified choke leave you much room for error at close ranges.

Later, you might want to go up a couple of shot sizes and screw in a tighter choke tube—modified with steel or tungsten blends, improved modified or full with bismuth. That will put more pellets on target, resulting in cleaner kills and fewer lost birds.

There's no single correct answer—waterfowling is too varied for that. We think the best approach is to choke your gun and choose your load to the situation, and err on the side of too much choke and too big of a pellet. The closest thing to an all-around combination would be No. 2 steel shot through a modified choke.

Finally, know your own limitations. If birds are cruising by, giving you 45-yard crossing shots, and you aren't proficient at those, you probably shouldn't shoot regardless of the shell you have in your gun. Every year, we see people hunting with chokes and loads that they say can kill birds cleanly at 60 yards or more, and at times it seems that some choke and ammo makers are promoting long shooting. Well, a 60-yard shot at a duck is a stretch even for Anthony, one of the finest shots in the world. So should an average hunter who doesn't practice often expect to make one? That person is better off with open chokes and waiting for a good, close shot.

There's no point in planning for a shot you can't make, so pick your choke and load based on your own ability.

FIELDCRAFT

The better you are at fieldcraft, the easier your shots will be. It's as simple as that.

For ducks and geese, fieldcraft includes (but isn't limited to) hiding, setting decoys, and calling. Do a good job with those, and most of your shots will be at birds sailing in on cupped wings, making their final approach for landing. That's about as easy as it gets. Trip up on any one of those things and you're going to be shooting at wary, flaring birds at longer distances—if you're lucky enough to get any shots at all.

There have been whole books written on setting decoys and calling waterfowl, not to mention numerous videos. If you want good instruction on calling waterfowl, just look up Primos Hunting on YouTube—Will has a host of videos that will start you off in the right way and give you some pro-level tips once you've mastered the basics. There's also plenty out there on decoy setups. For the purposes of this book, we'll focus on hiding and how to shoot from a hidden position.

This is what you want the ducks to see as they fly toward your decoys—no hunters in sight.

The first rule of thumb is that if you think you're hidden well enough, think again. Add some more brush to your blind, or pull on a camo mask under your hat. Ducks and geese have remarkable eyesight, and they can pick out the gleam of sunglasses or the flash of a hunter's face from a long way away. You almost can't have enough concealment.

That includes a roof over your head. Anthony hates hunting without one. If you're hunting out of a pit or other permanent blind, you usually have a roof, but if you're using a portable blind or building one of your own, figure out a way to rig some cover. Above all, you don't want square or round dark black holes staring up at the sky. That will flare birds as surely as a badly blown call.

Position yourself and your buddies so that when you do shoot, you're in the best position to connect. Left-handed shooters should set up on the right end of the blind, and righties on the left. That lets them swing more easily at birds flying by. Shooters in the middle are restricted to shots directly in front, or if it's safe, directly out the back. Make sure you have a good opening so that when you shoot, you're not screened in by brush. You must have a clear lane for shooting!

If you use layout blinds, try to set up with the wind at your back so the birds will be landing in front of you. Right-handed shooters should angle their blinds slightly right and left-handers slightly left to maximize their range of movement.

Keep your head down and stay still. Movement—even by a hunter dressed in camo from head to toe—spooks ducks. The person who's calling should be able to tell you where the birds are before you stand up and shoot. Sometimes, if you're hidden well, you can peep through the brush or look down at the water to see the birds' reflections. If not, trust the caller. That person also should determine when you should shoot—or, if multiple people are calling, pick one experienced hunter to make the call. Over the years, we've gone out with many "experienced" hunters who fail to hide and stay still. Remember, if you can see the birds, they can see you! Nothing ruins a chance at a big flock more than a hunter who stands up and fires too soon—maybe one bird drops while the others flare away and make their escape unharmed.

Position yourselves so you're in the best position to shoot, and be ready to pick up your gun as you stand.

Unless you're in a layout blind, stand up to shoot. You'll shoot better, and it's safer as well. One of the scariest situations we've seen came when an older hunter who was struggling to stand decided to fire his gun from his seat in the pit blind. The muzzle went off only two feet from another hunter's head. His hearing was damaged permanently, but if the gun had been pointed just a few inches in the wrong direction, the consequences could have been far worse.

Finally, remember that most hunters are too slow to get up and too fast to shoot. Try to pick out a duck or goose before you stand to shoot, but even if you haven't, stand up quickly. Then take your time, focusing on a good, solid gun mount and a good focus on the bird's head or beak. You'll be pleased with the results.

CALLING THE SHOT

On some days and in some situations, knowing when to shoot or "calling the shot" is the most important part of a successful day on the marsh or in the field. When done properly, it lets you and your hunting partners capitalize on your opportunities and, ideally, enjoy some easy shooting. Done wrong, and you're trying to knock down birds that flare at the limit of ethical shooting range or beyond. It can be the difference between taking several birds from a single flock or watching them all fly away.

The first step is deciding who will call the shot for your group. Pick the person with the most experience, a person who understands his or her own capabilities as well as the capabilities of the others in the blind and knows when the birds are in range for everyone, not just the most accomplished shooter. In the perfect world, that person is also the best caller in the group and can "work" the birds while the other hunters are keeping their heads down and hiding.

The caller also can make or break the hunt for the rest of the group—he should consider passing up some shots to work the birds in a little bit better, giving more opportunities to the rest of the crew.

The caller also needs to understand just how the birds are working on a particular day, and that requires a good deal of experience. If the birds circle several times and then keep going, you need to recognize that and perhaps call the shot a bit earlier if the birds are within ethical range. If you don't, you may not get any chances. If you do, you might take a few birds out of a couple of flocks—and that's enough for a memorable day.

Taking shots at birds that are beyond your capacity is never a good idea, and an experienced hunter knows that. At best, you educate birds that might avoid your decoys in the future. At worst, you put a pellet or two in the guts of a duck or goose, condemning it to a painful death later.

In other conditions, you'll call the shot differently. Say you've got a gale blowing from behind you, and the ducks are fighting to get close to your decoys. Wait and let them get close! Shoot too soon and they will flip on the wind and escape; shoot at the right time and you may be well on your way to a limit.

And if you've got the wrong wind or no wind, or the sun is shining and the birds are pulling out or flaring, you must decide if you're going to call the shot and kill what you can kill, or wait just a little longer. Anthony errs on the side of calling the shot, because on a tough day, you're never sure how many chances you'll have.

What if you're one of the other hunters in the blind? Keep your head down and trust your buddy. He should be telling you where the birds are, and to get ready to stand and shoot. Have your gun in your hands, but keep the safety on!

When you get the call to "take 'em," get up as quickly as you can, and then take your time picking out a bird and making a good clean gun mount, and fire as you concentrate on the bird's beak or head. Above all, know your abilities, and don't take unethical shots. If there's a shot that gives you trouble—say, a high incomer or big crosser—get out on the clays course and learn it before next season begins.

Summary:

- Calling the shot is an art, not a science, and can vary from day to day.
- The person who calls the shot should generally be the most experienced hunter and a competent caller. He or she should know how to read the birds and anticipate what they should do.
- The right moment to shoot is determined by the way the birds are working and by the hunters' abilities.
- With better shooters, it's easier to call the shot. With less-experienced shooters, be more cautious, and make sure the birds are in range.

SAFETY

Waterfowl hunting is the most social hunting there is. You sit next to your friends in the blind, sipping coffee and talking while waiting for the next flock to arrive. At the same time, it's the most chaotic. Watch a pod of teal catch a blind full of hunters by surprise—the coffee cups go flying while the hunters grab their guns and launch a broadside at swerving, flaring ducks. With so much going on, it's easy for something to go wrong. Here are some ways to prevent it.

1. **Don't load your gun until shooting time.** There's no good reason to be ready to shoot before you can legally do so. It also should be obvious that guns should be empty while you're carrying them to and from the blind.

2. **Keep your safety on until you're raising the gun to shoot.** Many hunters—too many—click off their safety as soon as birds start working their spread. Don't. If the birds fly away and you forget to put the safety back on, you're asking for trouble. If the gun is leaning in a rack or corner, a rambunctious dog could knock it over, potentially causing an accident. Learn how to flick off your gun's safety as you mount the gun, and check it periodically during the hunt to make sure it's on. Finally, make sure your hunting buddies put their safeties on after shooting. Don't worry about hurt feelings.

3. **Keep your finger off the trigger until you're about to shoot.** Cold weather and gloved hands can be a recipe for an accidental discharge.

4. **Shoot "your zone."** Each hunter in your blind should have a predetermined zone of fire and should pass up shots outside of it. In most cases, the safe zone is between ten and two o'clock. Hunters on the outside edges have more leeway, but under no circumstance should anyone shoot across or over another hunter. You can permanently damage your partner's hearing, or worse. One of us has even seen one hunter blow off the end of his buddy's gun barrel by swinging too far to the left.

Whether you are shooting from a pit blind or a standing blind,
you must pay attention to safe shooting zones.

5. If you turn around to take a shot behind you, **make sure the gun barrel is pointing straight up as you turn.** Do not sweep the line of hunters in your blind.

6. **Don't shoot a cripple if a dog or another hunter is trying to retrieve it.** Even if you think you have a clear shot, funny things can happen and pellets can ricochet. The only person shooting "over the dog" should be the hunter who owns it. Taking a shot at a cripple with the dog on its heels is sometimes necessary when hunting a river or stream with a heavy current. It is the task of an experienced shooter who is also the dog owner.

7. Let someone—probably the most experienced hunter in the group—"call the shot," and **don't shoot until you get the go-ahead.** On singles and doubles, there's no need for everyone to stand up. Take turns. It's safer, and you'll know without a doubt whether you shot the bird.

8. **Be familiar with your gun and what ammunition it can safely fire.** Let's say you're shooting a 12-gauge autoloader chambered for 3-inch shells, and you forget your ammo or run out. You ask your partner for some extra shells, and he hands you some 3½-inch magnums. That's an accident waiting to happen. Similarly, a 20-gauge shell mistakenly loaded into a 12 gauge can slide down the barrel and lodge there—and the next shot could blow up your gun.

9. **If you fall in the mud**—as you will eventually—**make sure your shotgun muzzle is clear.** Mud can cause a dangerous blockage in barrels. A quick swab with a cleaning rod can get you back in action.

10. **Wear eye and ear protection.** It's especially important in waterfowling, where on good days you may shoot a lot—and your buddies may, too. Inside a blind, a gunshot can seem even louder. Anthony wasn't taught to wear ear protection while hunting, though he always did while shooting clays. Today, when he takes his kids, he brings along ear protection for them. If you choose not to wear ear protection and risk damaging your hearing, that's up

to you. But if you bring kids along, teach them the right way and let them make their own decisions later.

11. **Always remember—you can't take back a shot.** Pass up a marginal shot if there's any doubt. You can always shoot another duck, but you can't undo a mistake.

DOUBLES AND TRIPLES

Shooting doubles on ducks and geese can be important. If you only have two or three flocks of ducks commit to your decoys on a given morning, you had better be able to take a couple from each group if you want to pluck a limit later that day. With Canada geese, shooting a double often means that you're done for the day and you can leave the field, allowing more birds to eat and loaf near your blind unmolested. That can pay off with another good hunt in that same location.

Too often, the flock flies away, leaving behind only one or two birds as well as a group of frustrated hunters who know they flubbed the best chance of the day, maybe the season. Let's talk about how to prevent that.

It may seem odd, but the secret to shooting doubles or triples on waterfowl is to take your time. Too often, hunters shoot too quickly, blazing at the flock in front of them and not taking the time to pick out individual birds and make a good shot. Pick out the bird you will shoot first, then lock your eyes on a part of that bird such as its head or the color on its chest—this will get you zeroed in on one bird. You can't kill a double without first killing a single, so make sure you do that before moving on to the next bird. And make sure the first bird is dead before you move on to the next. If you've only winged it, there's a good chance that duck will get away before the smoke clears and your dog starts making retrieves.

Second—if ducks are just hanging there in front of you with their feet down and wings spread, the way hunters see them in their dreams, don't shoot the closest bird! Chances are good that your partner will shoot at that one, too, and you'll shred that duck while the farther birds flare away. We've seen flocks of a dozen birds work the decoys perfectly, only to have three hunters double up on a pair of birds. You don't want to be those hunters. Talk to each other so you don't shoot the same birds.

Instead, pick out a duck toward the back of the flock for your first shot. Once you shoot it, the closer birds should still be in easy range and you can pick out another one. Anthony and his brother, Mike, have a system where Anthony works on the back of the flock while Mike—a fast and instinctive shooter—cleans up in front. It works so well that the brothers often take six birds out of a single bunch, but it only happens through teamwork.

This strategy also works if you're hunting alone. If you shoot a big Canada at thirty yards, any bird closer than that should be easy pickings for you. If you shoot the closest bird, the group will flare, giving you nothing to shoot at but feather-padded backsides. Unless you break a wing in that situation, the bird will probably fly away with a pellet or two in its guts and will die painfully that night or the next.

All the rest of the strategies for shooting are the same: Pick out a single bird, and try to focus on a detail like an eye, a bill, the white patch on a Canada's cheek, a mallard drake's green head, or the coppery sheen of a bull canvasback's head. Stand up quickly, but don't rush your shot. Point at the bird instead of aiming at it. Once the first bird is dead, shift your eyes to find the second bird, looking beyond the barrel. Get the same focus on the head or bill and pull the trigger. Then sit back and smile while your dog brings back your double.

ETHICS AND SPECIAL SITUATIONS

Nothing's more emblematic of waterfowl hunting than the green head of the drake mallard. A strap of glistening drakes hanging from a game strap next to a wet Labrador is an image emblazoned on the mind of almost every duck hunter. If any nonhunter were asked to name a wild duck species, chances are the response would be "mallard."

Some hunters try not to shoot mallard hens, even though they can legally be part of a daily limit. In fact, mallards are the only duck whose limits specifically mention gender; the drake's plumage is so different from the hen that it usually can be identified in flight. Waterfowl scientists say there's no reason not to shoot hens: they can be harvested without harming the population. But the feelings of many duck hunters are summed up simply: hen ducks in the freezer don't lay eggs the next spring.

Regardless of the science or your opinion, there are a couple of good reasons to single out drake mallards if you can:

1. Waiting to pick out a drake, or to "see green," means you will see the ducks better before you decide to shoot. The better you can see, the better you will shoot.
2. The green head makes a superb spot to lock onto as you raise your gun and fire, again increasing your chances of success.
3. Shooting only greenheads can extend your time in the field and, with time, can become a source of deep satisfaction. It can be a goal in and of itself, just like the fly angler who chooses to fish only with a dry fly.

Of course, all this is easy to say if you're blessed with a good hunting spot in a mallard flyway. Many hunters scan empty skies for hours, and if the only reasonable shot of the day happens to be at a mallard hen, should they pass it up? We're not about to argue that they should, so long as it's legal. Nor do we condemn those who make a mistake and shoot a hen. People who say they've never misidentified a duck in flight probably haven't done a lot of duck hunting. Follow the regulations and enjoy yourself!

As you read elsewhere in this book, we're big proponents of hunting with a dog. They add fun to the adventure, find more game for you, and hopefully, bring it to hand. We'd go even further when it comes to waterfowling: A good retriever is essential.

By and large, ducks and geese are big, tough birds that are shot at slightly longer distances than upland birds, and often over water. A wader-clad human is not going to run down a crippled gadwall frantically paddling for cover. The best-case scenario in that situation is that the hunter gets close enough to finish the duck with a well-placed shot

Many waterfowlers won't even consider hunting without a dog.

on the water. Even then, the duck might have gotten into water so deep that a human can't reach it without swimming.

Diving ducks on big water? Unless you have a boat ready to chase down and scoop up cripples, you'll lose far too many. Do you want to shoot a limit of ducks and only bring home a couple? We surely don't.

There are some exceptions to the rule. Flooded-timber hunting offers close shots in very shallow water, which makes recovery some-what easier. Nor will wounded ducks travel very far if they're shot over a dry-field decoy spread, as is common in Canada and the Plains states. You'll likely recover almost all your birds even without a dog.

Yet for many hunters, the dog is one of the most important elements of duck hunting. Besides their obvious worth in the field, duck dogs like Labrador retrievers are loyal and gentle pets, equally at home and in the blind. Offseason training is fun, and addicting to some people who wind up participating in field trials. We all know Labrador owners who swear that if they had to choose, they'd leave their shotgun behind before they'd leave their dog.

Our bottom line: Get a dog, or make friends with people who have them.

Another point or two about recovering birds: Even if you have a dog, you may find yourself in a situation where you need to "swat" a bird on the water to kill it before it escapes. For that, smaller shot is excellent at closer ranges—No. 5 or 6 steel, or the same size in bismuth. It'll give a denser pattern and increase the odds of hitting the bird in the head and killing it quickly.

WHEN IT'S COLD

Cold-weather hunting creates a special challenge. Gloves, heavy coats, and multiple layers can make it hard to mount the gun properly, let alone make the shot. There are a few things that can help:

- **Thin layers:** A good thermal undershirt covered by a wool shirt and a sweater will keep you very warm, particularly in an enclosed blind.
- **A snug-fitting outer jacket:** This will help you mount your gun without it catching on your clothes.
- **A shorter recoil pad on your gun:** The gun that fits well while you're in shirtsleeves may be too long when you're heavily padded for the winter. Swap a 1-inch pad for a ½-inch pad and you'll probably be pleased.
- **Hand warmers:** Hand warmers in pockets and fingerless gloves keep your trigger finger warm and limber. If it's especially cold, look for mittens with flaps that fold back, freeing up your fingers to take a shot.

Shoot low at birds on the water. If you aim at the head and the gun patterns slightly high, you may miss the bird entirely. Aiming low is a better bet, as some pellets may even skip off the water and hit the bird. And whatever you do, if a dog is anywhere near the duck, don't shoot!

(As an aside, we believe strongly that birds should be shot in the air whenever possible. Ground-pounding and water shots may be legal in some cases, but they're not very sporting. Save the water shots for cripples that otherwise might get away. Otherwise, pass them up.)

PRACTICING

Some waterfowl shots are easy. Will spent years shooting mallards fluttering through flooded timber, and he did very well. The problem was, he was aiming at the ducks. They were so close and moving so slowly that he could line them up with the bead on the end of his barrel and pull the trigger.

Crossers were another story. A teal ripping through the decoys, a flock of gadwall crossing at 30 yards, or a flaring mallard that didn't quite finish—all were usually safe from Will. That is, until he learned how to point his shotgun instead of aiming it.

As we explained previously, shooting a shotgun is a lot like driving a car. You see the metal hood under your nose, but you don't pay attention to it. Treat your barrel the same way. Forget about the bead on the end. In fact, take it off if you feel like it. It won't hurt your shooting and may help you break a few bad habits.

Think of lead not as a sight picture but as a relationship to the bird. You're either on the bird with no lead, a little bit in front of it, or way in front of it. The amount is determined by the angle, distance, and speed of the target. A slow quartering bird doesn't need very much lead, but a fast-flying diving duck presenting a true crossing shot at 35 yards does. If you look at your barrel, you're going to struggle with those.

You want to learn how to look at a target and get a feel for how much lead is required, whether you're starting your gun on or in front of it, or swinging through it from behind. You can't get that from a book, so you're going to have to get out to a clays course and shoot.

Much of the practice we described in the chapter on dove hunting holds true for waterfowl hunting as well. Trap doesn't help much unless you are used to jump-shooting ducks off creeks and ponds. Skeet will help you improve on crossing and quartering shots within about 25 yards, a reasonable distance for decoying birds. But to truly practice the full gamut of waterfowl shots, head to a sporting clays course.

You don't have to shoot every target presentation. Rabbit targets bouncing along the ground are fun but don't do much for a duck hunter. Nor do going-away shots like those you see on a trap field.

But short, medium, and long crossing targets are excellent practice for ducks and geese. If you can find targets being launched off a tower, that's even better. Incoming shots, particularly the ones that settle into the ground within 30 yards of the shooting stand, are good practice for decoying birds. Low, fast targets from any angle will remind you of diving ducks, like redheads and bluebills.

Towers also give you the chance to practice high shots as incomers and outgoers. They may seem intimidating at first, but a high bird directly above you has all its vitals exposed and can be killed very easily if you know the proper techniques. Hunters also drastically overestimate height, passing up a 30-yard duck directly overhead shot to blaze away at a 45-yard crosser. Trust us, the overhead shot is easier to execute and is often more lethal as well.

Long crossers will give a better idea of just how hard it is to consistently kill birds cleanly beyond 35 yards. Remember, a "chipped" clay target is scored "dead" even though you only hit it with a couple of pellets. A duck or goose hit with only a couple of pellets isn't likely to fall unless you strike its head or break a wing. Even then, it may be a difficult retrieve. If long-range practice persuades you to pass up some marginal shots, that's a good thing. If it helps you hit more birds that are a little closer, that's also good.

If you find a swiftly rising target, you might spot the resemblance to a flaring teal climbing away from your decoys. A dropping shot is another way to practice shooting decoying birds—or, perhaps, putting a finishing shot into a wing-tipped duck plummeting to the water. Knowing how to shoot dropping targets has helped us recover more than a few wounded birds that otherwise might have gotten away.

If you have your own (clay) trap or traps, you can set up other good scenarios. With a remote, you can safely throw crossing and incoming targets, and you can set up your layout blinds to practice sitting up and shooting quickly. You also could sit on a dove stool to practice standing up and shooting. Just make sure to keep your safety on until you're about to fire, the same as you would in a hunting situation.

Some shooting ranges might let you shoot from a layout blind or stool, but ask permission first! It's not a common practice, and if the club manager says no, don't argue. You still should get out and work on the club's targets.

Finally, a very underrated skill among waterfowl hunters is the ability to gauge distances. As we mentioned, hunters frequently overestimate the height of birds flying directly overhead and pass up very makeable shots. But they often underestimate the distance of decoying birds and crossers.

Try to find out the distances of various targets where you practice. You'll probably recognize that for many people, a "long" shot is closer to 35 yards than it is to 50 . . . and 50 yards is an awfully long way if you're trying to hit something with a shotgun.

You don't have to shoot to get better at distance estimation, though. If you're on a walk, try to estimate the distance to a tree, or a mailbox, or a boulder. Then pace it off and see how close you are. If you have a life-size "robo" decoy, put it up in your back yard and look at it from various distances and angles. It might not be perfect, but you'll soon recognize just how small a mallard appears at a true 40 yards.

Nor do you have to shoot to get better at mounting your gun. A few minutes every day mounting your empty gun before a mirror can make you smoother and more efficient in the field. You also can practice getting up from a layout blind, controlling your muzzle, and mounting the gun on a spot on the wall. Practicing from a layout blind is an especially good idea if you don't regularly do sit-ups and could stand to lose a few pounds.

ANTHONY'S TIPS FOR DUCK HUNTERS

Concealment is the most important thing. If you have great opportunities and lots of them, you can get away with not being hidden very well. But it's always more fun when you trick the birds and they work extremely well, landing almost on top of you. So cover up. Have a roof over your head if possible, and take the extra time to put more grass and brush on your blind.

If you're hidden well, the birds are going to come in closer and give you better opportunities, increasing your chances of success. Even though I'm very experienced and feel confident in my ability to shoot flaring birds, I still want to take the extra time to make sure that I've done everything I can to improve my hide. I can't emphasize it enough.

You can spoil the best blind in the world by sticking your head up at the wrong time. A shiny face will flare ducks and geese as surely as a mirror flashing in their face. Keep your head down, and don't look up.

Sometimes you can see the ducks or geese reflected in the water. That's a good way to keep track of the birds without staring up into the sky. If you can't do that, you can designate a person to keep an eye on the birds and to call the shot. Everyone else should be hiding as well as possible.

Even if you have the perfect blind, sometimes the birds will pass you up and land somewhere close by. Pick up and move to that location if possible. Animals are creatures of habit, so if the ducks are landing elsewhere, it's because they have food there or feel safe there. Don't wait to see if they change their mind—get over there!

In other situations, birds will land just outside your decoys. Think about making an adjustment as soon as you notice a trend—change up your decoys, check your blind, see if the sun is throwing a suspicious shadow on the ground. Once a few birds pass you by, odds are good that others will follow.

Will might disagree, but I don't think calling is as important as many people think it is. A good caller makes a difference, but average callers who call too much probably scare off as many birds as they attract.

You don't need to call that much. I think you can call more if you're proficient, but if you listen to the very best callers—people like Will—they call only when necessary. You must learn how to read the birds. If they're acting like they're about to pull away, call. If they're working your decoys or checking out your spread, quiet down. And if they're right on top of you, don't call. You'll only draw more attention to yourself, making it more likely that the birds will spot you and escape.

Motion decoys are a huge advantage, whether they're spinning-wing models or the type that spurt water to mimic feeding ducks. They might not matter so much if you're in a small pond or a wood duck hole. But on big water with passing birds—the type of duck hunting I do in New Jersey with my brother and buddies—motion decoys can be the difference between success and an empty strap.

Just make sure that your local regulations allow motion decoys. If they're banned where you are, try an old-fashioned jerk string to put a bit of movement on the water.

All waterfowl hunting boils down to capitalizing on your opportunities. That means making the right decisions on when to stand up and shoot, making a good clean gun mount, and pulling the trigger at the right moment.

Most hunters miss their moment of opportunity and don't mount the gun well enough to take the bird when it's in the best spot. This goes back to being well hidden. By hiding well, you can create a bigger window of opportunity for you to make the shot. That's why it's so important.

CHAPTER 9

TURKEYS

Spring turkey hunting is one of Will's passions. Maybe it's because a gobbler is one of the wariest of quarries, with exceptional eyesight and a range of vision that exceeds 180 degrees. Or maybe it's because it's the first hunting season to open in each calendar year, a chance to get out in the woods after a long winter. There's no doubt that great skill is necessary to learn how to locate a turkey and figure out a plan to shoot him as he comes to your call.

The shooting itself has more in common with deer hunting than any other kind of hunting with a shotgun. If you've done it right, your first shot on a turkey is at a stationary or barely moving target, and you line up your sights on the turkey's head and neck and squeeze off a shot like you're shooting a rifle rather than a shotgun. In other words, you *aim* your gun at stationary targets like turkeys, as opposed to *pointing* your gun at birds in the air. Knowing the difference is key.

The challenge is to figure out how to be in position to make that shot without the gobbler figuring you out. If you've never done it, believe us when we say it's harder than it sounds!

FIELDCRAFT

There are plenty of little tricks to getting the best possible shot at a turkey. It starts when you sit down in the woods. If you're a right-handed shooter, angle your body so that your left shoulder points toward where you expect the turkey to be. Lefties should do the opposite. This gives you a range of more than 180 degrees to shoot the gobbler, whether he's coming from your right or from your left.

Here's how Will likes to set up for turkeys—ready to point his gun in an arc of more than 180 degrees.

This might not matter so much if you're ambidextrous, but other people (including Will) are extremely dominant in one eye and struggle to shoot off both shoulders. Will takes extra care to set up properly, making sure he's aware of any saplings, vines, or other obstructions between him and where he expects the turkey to appear. Saplings, vines, and brush have saved more turkey lives than you'd believe!

Prop your shotgun on your knee, with your stock resting on your chest or in your lap. Just don't let the barrel point up where it can easily be seen. Position your head so you're looking over the barrel—this allows you to see better.

Don't mount the gun fully, because if you put your cheek on the stock, you limit your vision and the turkey can slip up on you or by you. Be as comfortable as possible: once the turkey starts making his approach, you can't move. You can't move your head or your hands, because he'll surely spot you. You want to be sure that you can make your final move to aim your shotgun while the turkey can't see you.

You might have to wait to make your final move until the turkey gets behind a tree, but be careful—the turkey's eyes are incredible. If the turkey is more than a few yards or so from the tree, he can see you. If he's close to a large tree, you can make your move. But be careful that another turkey with the gobbler doesn't spot you and sound the alarm.

Point your gun on the edge of the tree and let him take a few steps past the tree if possible. Hopefully his head will be up, and you can shoot him at that point, because that's when he's most vulnerable. If his head isn't up, you may need to yelp or cluck at him softly with a mouth call.

Put the shotgun sight or bead on the turkey's wattles, the fleshy bumps on the base of his neck. Don't aim at the top of his head; that will send more than half your pattern over his head. You want your pattern to bust the turkey's head and break his neck. You need to know exactly where your barrel is and line up your sights on the gobbler. In that sense, shooting turkeys has more in common with shooting a rifle than it does with shooting ducks or doves.

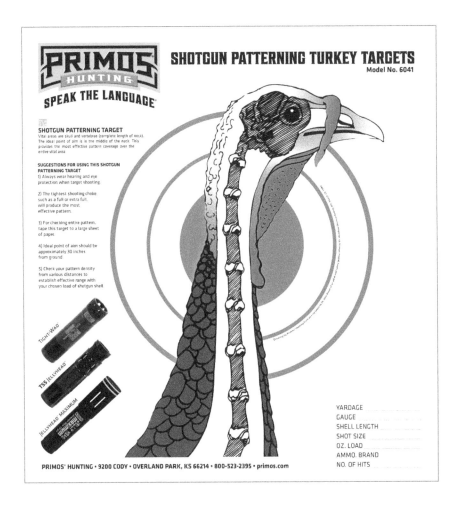

This target will help you understand how important it is to hit a turkey in the head and neck.

Get better at estimating distances, or use a laser range finder to help you recognize when a turkey is in range. Even though ammunition companies say their premium shells can kill turkeys at 60 yards, Will believes you should try to shoot them at 40 yards or less. That gives you more margin for a slight aiming error, and improves your chances for a clean kill.

EQUIPMENT

Today's high-density loads such as TSS (tungsten super shot) have made it possible to hunt turkeys with every gauge of shotgun, even the tiny .410 caliber. Because turkey hunting is often a one-shot game, many hunters have even gone to specialized small-gauge guns. Others set up smaller-scale youth guns for turkeys, finding that the shorter stocks and barrels are easier to handle and shoot from a sitting position, the way most people set up for turkeys.

Will believes a second shot is a good idea, so he prefers doubles, pumps, and semiautomatics for his turkey hunting. Though plenty of turkeys are shot by hunters using guns featuring blued metal and glossy walnut stocks, he recommends a camouflage finish to give you every possible chance of hiding from a turkey's laser-sharp vision. Make sure the gun throws a tight pattern at the distances you plan to shoot—you want multiple hits on the turkey's head and neck.

Many turkey hunters set up their guns like rifles, seeking maximum accuracy with their tight patterns. You'll even see turkey guns with rifle sights, Red Dots, or low-power scopes. Will prefers a simple ventilated rib with beads, as he believes he can shoot that setup very accurately but isn't handicapped when he shoots a running or flying gobbler. But he understands that's a personal preference. "If you like the red dot, if you like rifle sights—it's all about execution," he says. "You're calling up that gobbler and making him hunt you. He stands there looking for you, and you aim at his wattles and let him have it."

Will likes to shoot his pet side-by-side shotguns at turkeys, and he also has a 20-gauge youth model shotgun that he uses at times. The shorter stock and barrel make it easier to handle from a sitting position in the woods. Will also has equipped his 20 gauge with a suppressor and uses subsonic ammunition to protect his ears. You want to be able to hear a turkey making his way toward you, but you also don't want your ears to take the blast from a short-barreled shotgun.

As for ammunition: Will likes TSS, the densest shot currently available. Tiny No. 9 pellets made from TSS are as heavy as much larger lead pellets and hit just as hard—and there's more of them. Will's seen TSS patterns that would put 50 or more pellets into a turkey's head and neck at 40 yards, and that is a very dead turkey. Will also swears by the special TSS shells handloaded by Ray Filogomo of the Nitro Company in Mountain Grove, Missouri.

If there's a drawback to TSS, it's cost. Some shells cost more than $10 each. But you don't shoot much in turkey hunting, and even if you shoot a dozen patterning targets before the season, your ammo bill will still be lower than most of your other hunting expenses. You might as well go with the most effective shell possible—just don't try to stretch your shot too far. Know your gun's effective range and yours. And remember, stuff gets in the way of shot patterns, so make sure you have a clear line of shot to your gobbler.

If you can't shoot TSS or other tungsten-based shot (perhaps because you use an older gun, or you can't find any), then lead works. Will recommends copper-plated lead because it resists deformation and therefore patterns more tightly than other lead loads. He likes No. 5 shot and tries to keep his shots with lead within 40 yards. That's a good rule even for the tungsten loads. There's no worse feeling than taking a slightly-too-long shot and wounding a majestic gobbler that gets away. "A lot of guys want to see how far they can shoot a turkey, but when you do that, you're stretching," Will says. "Something's going to be in the way, or you're going to wound the turkey. You want to be patient until you are confident you have a lethal shot."

What's more important: the perfect gun, the perfect shell, or being the perfect hunter? Will says it's all important, but it's essential to pattern your turkey gun with the ammunition you think you should use. Primos makes a patterning target with the outline of a turkey's head and neck. Shoot patterns from a solid rest at 20, 30, and 40 yards, and see how many pellets strike the head and neck at each distance. Look for consistent strikes up and down the neck and determine the effective range for your ammo, your gun, and for you.

A final thought that doesn't relate directly to shooting but will pay off with easier shots: Wear good camo and keep still. Will swears by Mossy Oak Bottomland camouflage and has killed turkeys in every corner of the United States wearing it.

The right camouflage is a huge help because turkeys see so well. Will compares a turkey's head and neck to the periscope on a submarine—they can see almost anything around them and remain hidden from the hunter. If you move, the turkey will see you. That makes camouflage required from head to toe, including a face mask. And stay rock still while the turkey is coming into range. Then you can take your shot and pick up your prize.

SAFETY

Turkey hunting can be dangerous. You're swaddled in camo from head to toe, trying to make yourself invisible to a turkey—but that can make you invisible to other hunters as well. Then you or your partner are making sounds like a turkey, and in the worst-case scenario, an adrenaline-filled hunter will convince himself that there's a gobbler right where you are sitting and send a load of shot your way. So always positively identify the gobbler and his beard before you pull the trigger!

Taking care of your own safety starts with your setup. Put your back up against a tree, rock, or something else to hide and shield you while you are calling. Once there, stay there until your best judgment says the gobbler isn't coming—and remember, patience is best. Stay still and let the gobbler hunt for you.

Don't wear the gobbler's colors: red, white, and blue. Even a red bandanna peeking out of a pocket can look like part of a turkey to an excited hunter.

After you've killed your gobbler, drape him in florescent orange as you carry him out of the woods. You don't want someone to shoot at a bird you're carrying. Putting on an orange hat as you walk out of the woods isn't a bad idea, either.

Above all, make sure you know your target. See the turkey clearly before pulling the trigger, and *never* shoot at a sound or movement.

PRACTICING

Once you've got your turkey gun set up and patterning well, it's not a bad idea to try shooting some patterns from a hunting position. Sit down as you would in the field and set up your patterning target 20 to

30 yards away. You don't necessarily need to use your expensive TSS loads for this close practice; the purpose is to get you used to shooting from awkward positions. Then practice *slowly* moving the gun into position and shooting. Take shots off to your right, your left, and straight ahead.

You'll also get a better idea of how your gun patterns at closer ranges. It's one thing to shoot a gun off a sandbag rest, with your head locked down on the stock, and quite another to shoot when you've wrapped yourself into knots trying to get a clear shot at a big gobbler. This practice will help you learn the difference.

WHEN YOU CAN'T AIM

Will's friend Brad Farris is famous for shooting twice at turkeys. He'll forget to put his head down or something else that makes him miss his first shot. Then the turkey launches himself into the air, using those big drumsticks like a catapult on an aircraft carrier.

Brad immediately goes into instinct mode. He looks at the turkey's head, swings his gun, and shoots like he's picking off the world's largest quail. The turkey crumples to the ground with a broken head and neck.

"It's hilarious," Will says. "I can't tell you how many videos we've done with Brad Farris . . . he's a whole lot better wing shot than he is aiming a shotgun at a still target."

Will also remembers a time hunting with Ronnie "Cuz" Strickland in Tennessee. They called up a pair of gobblers, and for whatever reason, Will missed his first shot. Just like Brad Farris, he went into instinct mode, swung the shotgun, and rolled the running turkey with his next shot.

Those two stories explain why Will prefers beads on his turkey guns as opposed to rifle sights, scopes, or red-dot aiming devices. Occasionally, killing a turkey is more like wing shooting than rifle shooting—and you should be ready for that.

Brad Farris and a "two-shot" gobbler.

CHAPTER 10

DEER

Deer hunting is different. Unlike waterfowl or upland hunting, it doesn't require a lot of equipment or a dog—all you need is a firearm, bow, or crossbow, and some cartridges or arrows. Find a place to go, whether it's public land or private property, and you're in business. You don't even need a blind; just sit quietly at the base of a tree. (Of course, a blind or deer stand helps with concealment—and if you have one, use it.)

That low cost of entry is just one of the reasons why deer hunting is so popular across the United States. It also provides a lot of bang for your buck, no pun intended. If you are lucky enough to kill a deer, you'll have plenty of meat for the months ahead, whereas a limit of doves might not even feed a large family for one meal.

Deer also require a different approach than most other forms of shotgun hunting. Generally, with deer, you wait for a moment when the buck or doe is standing still or just barely moving, and you line up your sights on its body whether you're shooting a shotgun, rifle, compound bow, or crossbow. You're aiming at a stationary animal, as opposed to pointing at and swinging with a moving one.

There are exceptions to that, and that's the point of this chapter. We both have experience with stationary and running deer, and our insights will help you in the field.

FIELDCRAFT

Deer hunting has a great deal in common with turkey hunting, so go back and read our tips in the previous chapter on turkeys. Concealment and staying quiet is the key, and learning how to estimate distances is a vital skill for deer hunters regardless of what equipment they use.

You should do some scouting before the season to find trails frequented by deer, or to spot where they usually enter a field. That's where you want to set up, as deer are creatures of habit. If they come into the field from a certain location one day, it's a fair bet they'll do the same the next.

Pay attention to the wind, and be downwind of where you expect the deer to be. Deer have an exceptional sense of smell, and a whiff of a human will send them running. A deer will question its eyes or its ears, but it will not question its nose.

Rain is a different story. Deer take advantage of rain to move silently through the woods, as the wet ground muffles their steps. So if it's drizzly, it might be a good time to head to your blind. If you've got a roof over your head, you'll be dry and comfortable, and the deer will be on the move. The same thing will happen when a cold front is moving in or out of the area.

Since Anthony started taking his daughters hunting, he's come to appreciate an enclosed ground blind. "If the deer cannot see you in that ground blind, they will doubt themselves," he explains. "When they don't see you and don't smell you, they're not alarmed. It is amazing how close to a blind or box stand they can get when they don't smell or see you."

EQUIPMENT

Shotgun hunting for deer usually is done with heavy single projectiles called *slugs* or, in some cases, large pellets called *buckshot*. In many areas, shotguns are required for deer hunters, as the pellets and slugs don't travel as far as high-powered rifle cartridges.

Over the years, slug guns have advanced dramatically. A few decades ago, most hunters just used their regular shotguns with standard barrels. Maybe they clamped some rifle sights on the rib, or they just made do with their beads. In either case, accuracy was limited to about 65 yards.

Today, we have slug guns designed just for that purpose, with rifling cut into the barrels and either with open sights already installed or set up to add a scope. Some specialized slug guns are built on a bolt action, just like a rifle. This has made the 20 gauge a viable choice for deer, and some modern slug guns are accurate enough to kill deer consistently at 100 yards or more.

Shooting one of these guns is just like shooting a rifle, right down to taking a solid rest and squeezing the trigger. But make no mistake, you still need to practice shooting before the season.

If you're in a state where buckshot is legal or required, get out and shoot your gun with various chokes and loads, hoping to create a snug pattern of pellets in an area just slightly bigger than a pie plate at 40 or 50 yards. That's about the maximum practical range to *consistently* kill a deer with buckshot. Buckshot comes in different sizes; we recommend No. 1, 0, or 00. Larger pellets like 00 carry more energy, but there are fewer of them in a typical load.

Archery has advanced as well. Many archery hunters today are using crossbows complete with scope sights. And again, they're not that different from shooting a rifle. With practice, and a little bit of fine-tuning, you can ethically use crossbows out to about 60 yards, much farther than most people who use regular archery equipment.

Compound bows, which use pulleys to lighten the weight of the bow's pull, also can be sighted in like a rifle. Most compound archers use a system with a peep for a back sight and a series of pins set for specific distances. Instead of holding the bowstring with their fingers, they use special trigger-release mechanisms. Even so, their range is limited by the skill of the user. Even if an archer is competent out to 75 yards on the range, it's a good idea to limit shots to 40 yards or less because a deer can move before the arrow arrives on target.

Finally, there are the old-style "stick" bows—Will's favorites. In some ways, they're more like shotguns than you might imagine. There's no sight, so you must look at the spot you want to hit on the deer, usually behind the shoulder. You shoot with a great deal of trust, almost instinctively. If that sounds like wing shooting with a shotgun, it's because it is. The only difference is that ideally, the deer is standing still when you take your shot.

Again, the effective range of the traditional bow is based on the skill of its user. As a rule, knock off a few yards from your maximum range with a compound. Twenty yards is a good guideline.

There's lots more to learn about deer hunting equipment. Entire books have been written on the subject. That's not our goal for this book, so talk to other deer hunters about what works for them. Over time, you'll develop your own preferences. Just remember that equipment alone doesn't kill deer. We'd give pretty good odds that a good hunter with fair equipment will have greater success than a poor hunter with the best equipment available.

SAFETY

Every year, deer hunters die or are badly injured by not following safety instructions for handling guns and archery equipment. There are also many horrible accidents when a deer hunter falls out of a tree stand. We can't emphasize tree-stand safety enough. Always use a safety harness, and be careful climbing in and out of the stand. If you're hunting alone, make sure someone knows where you are, just in case you fall and can't move.

This should be obvious, but don't climb into a tree stand or box blind with a loaded gun. Climb into the stand first. If you're in a tree stand, haul up your unloaded gun or bow with a rope. Then you can load up.

Firearm deer hunting regulations generally require hunters to wear blaze orange—at minimum a hat, and in many instances a hunter-orange vest or other outer clothing. Check your state's laws. Blaze orange has been proved to reduce the number of hunting accidents, so wear it even if you think it makes you look like the Great Pumpkin.

Of course, all other safety rules apply. Above all, make sure of your target and be sure you have a safe backdrop. A shot at a deer silhouetted against the sky at the top of a ridge is almost always a bad idea. If you miss, your slug, buckshot, or arrows are going to sail over the ridge and land on the other side—and who knows who or what may be there?

GROWING UP WITH DEER

We grew up hunting deer. Anthony killed his first at age six and had been hunting with his father for a while before that. Some of his fondest memories involve sitting with his father or grandfather in a stand and killing his first deer with a bow and arrow, a shotgun, and a muzzle-loading rifle.

By age ten, he was hunting alone with both bow and shotgun. That may seem a little young in retrospect, but he had grown up on a hunting preserve, and his parents had drilled him and his brother on proper safety. They reasoned that the boys would be safer hunting on their own property than riding their bikes on a busy street.

The bow was a particular challenge. A ten-year-old can't handle the same bow as an adult, and so Anthony used a lighter one that barely met the legal requirements for hunting deer in New Jersey. He shot at a few deer before he connected with one, and practiced a great deal—an experience that he credits with developing his patience.

By the time he was fifteen, Anthony had been bitten by the waterfowl bug, and so walked away from deer hunting for a while. He's back at it today, for a very good reason: his kids. All three of his daughters join him on deer hunts, and it won't be long before his son comes along as well.

"It's a very good way to introduce kids to hunting, because it's easier than getting a little kid out walking in a marsh in cold weather or tromping in the field after a pheasant," he says. "We can pick the more reasonable days and go when the weather is nicer."

Fully prepared with drinks and snacks, Anthony takes his kids into a comfortable box blind that keeps them warm and hides any movement. If the deer aren't moving, they can watch other animals. If the girls are cold or really bored, they go home—there's always another day.

When Anthony does have success and kills a deer, the girls help him track it and, later, help dress it out in preparation for many memorable meals. It's a family tradition, one that Anthony hopes will continue for many generations to come.

Will started out deer hunting when it was all about horseback riders and dogs driving the deer toward the shooters in the woods. It certainly stirred the pot!

When he started, Will used a .30-30 Winchester Model 94 rifle, the classic "cowboy gun." Over time, he gradually fell in love with archery hunting—and that's a whole other story.

WILL'S FIRST BUCK

It was November 1963, and I was eleven years old. My uncle Billy took me to Ten Point, his deer club on Steele Bayou, north of Vicksburg, Mississippi. I had gone before, but this would be the first time I would be allowed to carry a gun and sit alone on a stand.

The stands were named for different states. My uncle Billy sat me down next to a big pin oak tree on the Georgia stand to wait. I had my prized Model 94 lever action, and I hoped with all my heart that a buck would try to sneak out of the coming commotion and give me an early shot. After all, everyone had put a dollar into a coffee can, and the first person to kill a buck would take the pot. This was all the encouragement needed to get everyone on their stand early.

The dogs jumped the buck not far from my stand, and here he came, running through the woods. I think I shouldered my rifle, but I'm not sure. I do know that I shot three times, working that lever action like *The Rifleman* on TV. I had never shot anything running, and for sure, I didn't shoot anything that day, either. Heck, I don't think I even looked at the sights. I just pointed and hoped.

The buck was a big, mature 10 point. I know because the guy on the next stand, Florida, killed him, and I got to put my hands on that beautiful buck's rack. Though I was happy for my fellow hunter, I hoped that one day I could make that running shot. Killing that big buck would have been a big deal for an eleven-year-old.

Will's first deer, November 1963.

After congratulating the hunter, I walked back to my stand, sat back down on my assigned spot up against that big pin oak, and settled down, hoping I might get another chance. Lo and behold, I looked up and spotted a spike buck slowly feeding on acorns, headed closer to my position. This was probably two hours after the big buck had run by, and everything had calmed down.

My uncle had taught me where to aim using pictures from *Outdoor Life* and *Field & Stream*. He taught me to wait for a shot that was broadside or a shot that gave my bullet the best chance to travel through the "boiler room," as he called it. Well, this spike buck was angling toward me and was about 30 yards away. I was very anxious and waiting for him to turn broadside. He turned his neck, looking back, and I had my chance. I lined up my sights on the base of his neck, and I pulled the trigger. He folded on the spot, the first of many deer to fall to my Winchester.

Five years later, I went with a high school friend, Rob Murphree, to Wayside, his hunting camp on Bell Island on the Mississippi River. Technically, it was in Arkansas. For safety reasons, the members didn't allow rifles. That meant you had to use shotguns with either a slug or buckshot.

I brought my old Remington 870 pump. A 12 gauge, it had no rib, just a modified 28-inch barrel with a single bead at the end. I practiced until I could hit with No. 1 buckshot out to about 50 yards.

Once again, I was assigned a stand and waited for the dogs and horsemen to push the deer toward us. Flocks of turkeys and quite a few deer poured past me, but I did not get a good shot at a buck. Things had calmed for a while, and then I saw him—an 8 point, sneaking through the woods, trying to get back to his hiding spot. As he sneaked by at 35 yards, I put the bead close behind his shoulders. At that distance, I knew my pattern would cover just behind the shoulder and the base of the neck. Sure enough, when I pulled the trigger, he collapsed. He was a young 8-point buck, two years old. But man was I proud—and I was surely glad that he hadn't been running!

Years later, I think about that first big buck. If I knew then what I know now—based on my experience with sporting clays and shooting at moving and flying targets—I would have focused on the spot where I wanted my bullet to hit and matched speeds with that deer as he ran through the woods, just ignoring the trees he was running by and making a shot count.

In the South, where Will lives, deer still are hunted with shotguns and buckshot.

And I would've put my open sights not behind his shoulder but on the front part of his shoulder. Given his speed, the distance, and my reaction time, that would have put the bullet 10 or 12 inches back into his body, right into his heart and lungs.

I've made that shot several times since that first encounter. You must know those things to shoot a running deer with a rifle or with a shotgun. Match speeds with the deer. Point your gun ahead of where you want to hit, and let her rip.

Just a few years ago, my friend Brad Farris and I saw a decent 8 point bed up in a grass field. A plan developed for Brad and his daughter Morgan to jump the buck and push him toward me. I would be waiting with my 16-gauge hammer gun, loaded with No. 1 buckshot. Those running shots were not so far out of reach anymore!

ARCHERY

It was 1963, and young Will Primos, age eleven, sat in a Jackson, Mississippi, movie house, waiting to see Alfred Hitchcock's *The Birds*. Before the feature, the theater operator showed a movie of the famed archer Howard Hill as he auditioned to take part in a movie about Robin Hood.

"I'd been shooting a little Ben Pearson bow made in Pine Bluff, Arkansas," Will recalls today. "So I'm watching Howard Hill, and I'm loving it."

Hill and other tryouts were challenged to slice a rope with their arrows. Hill hit the rope, but his arrows glanced off. So Hill stepped off the distance and went home and made a razor-sharp V-shaped broadhead that would catch and slice the rope instead of glancing off it. He also calculated how many times his arrow would rotate as it flew through the air. That way, he had a pretty good idea that the broadhead would cut that rope.

For Will, archery hunting for deer and elk is a passion.

"He draws back that long bow, angled like so. And—*tchu!*—he cuts the rope and gets the Robin Hood part," Will says. "So that was cool. Anyway, I learned to love the romance of the arrow from an early age of watching films of Howard Hill and Fred Bear and reading about Art Young and Saxton Pope."

Using flu-flus—arrows especially equipped with big feathers to limit their flight—Will learned how to shoot through trial and error. He even bought yew wood staves from Oregon and crafted his own longbows. After a time, he learned that shooting a traditional longbow or recurve bow had a great deal in common with shooting a shotgun: you stared at the point where you wanted your arrow to strike and kept your eyes on it through the shot. "Just like you focus on the target in sporting clays," he recalls. It was pointing, not aiming. He took a few lessons and got better and better.

"It's a lot of fun, and it's all instinctive," Will says. "Your eye and your brain anticipate the speed of the arrow, the speed of the animal, and the flight of the arrow. And you can shoot running stuff with a recurve. You can even shoot flying stuff with flu-flus."

In the mid-1970s, the compound bow emerged. It used a system of pulleys to allow archers to draw a heavier bow that propelled the arrows faster, with a flatter trajectory. Will hated them at first, thinking that it would destroy archery forever.

Then he wounded a few deer with his traditional bow and arrow and couldn't find them. That changed his perspective. Reasoning that a compound bow would help him kill deer more effectively, he picked one up and began practicing a new style: using a peep and pins to aim his arrow, much like shooting a slug gun or rifle.

"The secret to that is the trajectory of the arrow and knowing the distance to the target," Will says. "You're pulling back, the bow is perfectly vertical and you have perfect form, and you squeeze the release and follow through. It's as if the arrow almost comes flying out from your eye where you're aiming."

The flatter trajectory and the aiming system gave Will confidence with his compound bows out to about 70 yards, but keeping his shots to 40 yards or less was a huge advantage, as his team videoed deer hunts all over and archery elk hunts in the West. They became experts at calling in elk and taking them with well-placed arrows from compound bows.

Even today, Will is a highly competent archer with a compound bow. He attributes that to the ease of aiming a compound bow as opposed to the art of pointing a traditional one.

If a deer hears a bowstring, he's likely to duck as he coils his body to leap away.

Video also taught Will a trick or two. Frequently, arrows aimed at feeding deer fly high, either striking them high in the back or missing entirely. Some hunters blame their elevated tree stands for changing their arrow's intended trajectory.

But high-speed video at 30 frames per second revealed the real story: the deer were reacting to the sound of the bow and squatting to turn and flee. "A compound bow—let's say you're shooting arrows at 300 feet per second (which would be very fast). And with a recurve, maybe 155 feet per second," Will says. "But the deer can react faster, and he's a flight animal, so he hears the release of the arrow and he goes down and pushes to get away from that unnatural sound. So we learned to aim a little lower."

Another strategy came from Will's friend Paul Korn, one of the most successful bowhunters in history. Korn noticed, through his own video review, that deer ducked more aggressively and more often when their heads were down to feed.

"Paul says to shoot when the deer's head is up," Will says. "It's like the spring isn't cocked, so they duck less. Paul has videos with deer with their heads up and with their heads down and compares their reaction time. And when their head is up, the deer are not ducking the sound of the arrow near as much or as often. So wait till their heads are up, and you aim at the heart, right behind the crease of the leg. If the deer ducks, you're still going to hit him in the lungs."

What about aiming? Will recommends that bowhunters study deer anatomy and focus not on where the arrow will strike the body but where it will exit on the other side of the deer. Doing that will increase the odds of sending the arrow slicing through the vitals, or what Will refers to as "the goodie box." That's the surest way to a quick kill.

CHAPTER 11

PRACTICING WITH CLAY TARGETS

If you're reading this book, you obviously want to become a better shot. But let's be honest—reading a book doesn't automatically make you better at anything, much less a physical activity such as shotgun shooting. By the time you finish the book, hopefully you will have more knowledge than when you began. Now it's up to you to turn that knowledge into skill, and the way to do that is to practice.

It is possible to become a decent shot simply by hunting a lot, but it's not the fastest recipe of success. You need thousands of shots to reach your potential, and few of us have the time or opportunity to do that on live birds. The exception might be if you have the chance to hunt doves in South America, where the birds are considered pests.

There, you might be able to shoot 1,500 shells or more in a day—and after a few days, you'll probably be a much better wing shot. You'll also be sore, and a few thousand dollars poorer, but if you want to be a better wing shooter, there's nothing like it.

Most hunters today must learn on clay targets, either at an established shooting range or by using an inexpensive thrower on grounds where it is safe to do so.

Some hunters sneer at clay target shooting. They point out, correctly, that clay targets slow down after being launched from a trap, and that no clay target ever made can swerve like a blue-winged teal or mourning dove. And they say, with some merit, that some of the clay targets thrown at top-level sporting clays competitions have no resemblance to shots that an ethical hunter would take in the field.

Even so, clay targets are the best and most accessible way to learn how to shoot. We don't have better options—so if you want to improve, start shooting clays. You don't have to compete, you don't even have to keep score, but you do need to get out there.

How often? As often as you can. If you can get out every week to shoot 100 shells, that's great. If recoil isn't an issue and your strength is good, you can shoot more. If you can get out once a month, that's OK, too. The point is that you won't learn to shoot in one outing. You need repetition to build good habits and muscle memory.

We're not trying to turn you into a competitive target shooter by any means, though you may decide that clay shooting is fun in and of itself. Even if you can only shoot a few boxes of shells before hunting season begins, that will help you.

The simplest way to go about it is to go to the local clay shooting range and shoot sporting clays, skeet, or trap. Or buy a manual target thrower, or *trap*, that you can stake into the ground and launch targets by yanking a release cord. You can find them for $60 or so, maybe even less if you get lucky at a garage or estate sale. Lots of people got started that way. Just be sure that the person releasing the targets is standing behind the shooter and the shooter is off to the side of the trap. Safety concerns limit these traps to going-away and quartering targets—never take a shot that makes you point your gun anywhere near the person launching the clays.

The next step up is a battery-operated automatic trap, some of which have remote releases that will let you shoot on your own and safely shoot crossing shots and incomers. They go for a few hundred dollars and are worth the upgrade if you're going to shoot more than once or twice a year. Some people even buy a pair of automatic traps so they can practice shooting doubles.

If you don't have access to a gun club, you can shoot in an open field – just make sure you have enough room!

You'll need a bit of land to do this. Some state wildlife areas have spots set aside for target practice, and if you or your friends have rural property, you might be able to shoot there. Check local ordinances, and be sure that you allow at least 300 yards to make sure all the shot falls in a safe place. Raining pellets on the neighbors is a sure way to end your practice session quickly!

Most people wind up at an established range to shoot one of the clay target games. Here are the most popular:

- **Trap:** Up to five shooters stand in a line behind a trap that oscillates left and right. They shoot five single shots at individual targets before rotating to the next position.
- **Skeet:** Two traps, one set high off the ground and one set lower, throw crossing targets that shooters attempt from each of eight stations, and at some stations, they shoot doubles as well.
- **Sporting clays:** The newest target game, it's like golf with a shotgun—you shoot from different stations set along a course, and no two are the same. Most of the stations will have targets that resemble birds you might hunt, from doves to quail, and even skittering along the ground like a rabbit. There's a reason why this game sometimes was called "hunter's clays" when it came to the United States in the late 1980s.

All these games can provide good practice for hunters. Trap surely resembles birds flushing away from you, like sharp-tailed grouse or pheasants on the open prairie. Skeet was designed as practice for ruffed

Sporting clays offer shots at all angles, speeds, and distances.

grouse hunting, and it exposes you to everything from a target flying away overhead to a 25-yard crossing shot, perfect for a dove warm-up.

Most people who shoot trap and skeet for their own sake call for the target with the gun already at their shoulder. As a hunter, you can and probably should shoot from a low-gun start—just recognize that your scores probably won't be as high as those turned in by the specialized shooters.

Nor do you have to shoot regulation rounds at either game. If you're on a trap field, ask that the trap be locked down so it throws a consistent target instead of oscillating. Understand that a busy club probably can't do that for you. But if you talk to the club staff, you may find a solution.

Similarly, if you are trying to get better at shooting crossing targets, head to the skeet field but only shoot from stations 3, 4, and 5. You

One of Anthony's proudest moments came in 2016, when he became the first American to win the World Sporting Clays Championship.

can work on doubles by releasing the high-house and low-house bird simultaneously, or by releasing the second target when the shot is fired at the first—that's called a report pair in sporting clays.

Don't try to do this if other shooters want to shoot regular trap or skeet. Wait until you and your friends can get a field to yourselves.

Then there's sporting clays, which offers the widest variety of shots possible. Try to find a sporting clays facility that has a course with targets that aren't too extreme. If you don't hit targets, you won't have fun and you probably won't keep practicing. If you can't find an easier course, you have a few other options. One is to only shoot the easier stations—ask the members or club manager for suggestions.

If you're trying to improve, it's better to focus on specific targets at specific stations rather than to shoot the entire course, as you would do if you were shooting for score. Effective practice means breaking down the game into segments, just like any other sport. Golfers practice by going to the driving range and putting green, not by playing a round. Baseball players take batting practice and perform fielding and running drills. You should do the same—focus on fundamentals like seeing the bird well, mounting efficiently, and moving in sync with the bird.

Remember the science of shooting. Lead is determined by the target or bird's angle, distance, and speed. At the range you can learn by seeing various shots and building a memory bank. Over time you will understand how to generate lead while keeping your eyes on the target, not the barrel. Shooting is like any other sport: the more you practice, the better you become.

Finally, you can practice at home. Take an *unloaded* gun and pretend that the seam between a room's wall and ceiling is the path of a flying bird. Mount your gun slowly and move it along the seam, as you would while shooting at a bird. As you move around the room, the seam can represent any angle from a nearly straight-on incomer to a 90-degree crossing shot. It's a great way to work on pointing the gun and moving it smoothly.

Almost any kind of practice is better than none. Just remember that it won't pay off overnight. But after a while, you'll start to feel more comfortable and confident in the field, and there will be fewer and fewer occasions when you take a shot and the bird keeps on flying. Practice might not make perfect, but you can always get better.

CHAPTER 12

STARTING KIDS RIGHT

Will Primos with his good friend Reece McGlawn on the last day of the 2015 waterfowl season.

When should kids start shooting and hunting with a shotgun? Without question, it's more important to consider a child's maturity and size than their actual age. They need to be big enough to hold and control a gun, and they need to be able to follow directions and be safe. There are seven-year-olds who are ready and twelve-year-olds who aren't. The main thing is to make it safe, and make it fun!

Wait until your child wants to go. The worst thing you can do is to make children go shooting or hunting before they're ready. If that happens, their interest will wane quickly and they won't want to go back. After all, a duck blind can be uncomfortable even for adults when a cold wind is spitting sleet and rain. Imagine what it's like for a kid!

If a child wants to shoot, take them out and start showing them what the game is all about, including safety and respect for the gun. Get them a good pair of protective glasses and well-fitting hearing protection, and let them stand back and watch. Depending on the situation, you might let them push the buttons to launch the targets at the clay range. Above all, keep it fun and stop for the day when your child starts losing interest. That's a good strategy even after you transition to the hunting fields.

If they're very young or not sure about whether they want to shoot, let them try a BB gun. Anthony did this with his young daughters, setting up clay pigeons and letting the girls shatter them. It's a great transition to shooting clays for real—just make sure they point the gun rather than aim it.

Once kids do decide they want to shoot, it's crucial to get them the right equipment. It doesn't have to be perfect, but they can't shoot an adult's gun, and they can't shoot heavy shells. We've all seen kids who were handed a gun and shell that nearly knocked them backward when they fired. That's no way to encourage a kid, and in fact, it may scare them away for good.

To our minds, the best bet is a 28- or 20-gauge gas autoloader with a short stock, depending on the kid's size and strength. You can cut the stock length as short as 12 inches and add length with pads and spacers as the child grows.

Larger kids might be able to handle a 12-gauge gas-operated semi-automatic. Today's autos kick less than any other 12-gauge shotgun ever made. A gas-operated 12 paired with light one-ounce shells can handle any target and even some birds like dove and quail. If heavier shells are needed, the gas gun's lower recoil is a huge benefit.

Avoid a .410 shotgun, except for unique applications such as gun handling instruction and practice and shooting stationary targets. The shells are expensive, and the little gun can frustrate even the best shooters. A 28-gauge is almost as soft shooting, particularly if you choose a gas-operated auto, and is far more efficient.

We'd also caution against cheap guns, including inexpensive over/under shotguns. They simply aren't as reliable as a good autoloader, and they do nothing to soak up recoil. Many parents go this route with the best of intentions, but they wind up with a gun that kicks too hard and won't hold up to a lot of shooting. A good used gun is better than a poorly made new one.

Some people argue that a break-action gun is safer, but with proper instruction and supervision, an autoloader is as safe as any firearm. We're also wary of single-shot shotguns with exposed hammers. It's all too easy for the hammer to slip out from under a child's small thumb, especially in the cold and rain, causing an accidental misfire. In addition, most single-shots are very light and recoil quite a bit. If that exposed hammer kicks back into the shooter's face or hand, you've got a real problem.

What about a pump? There's nothing wrong with one, if you make sure it fits the child and isn't too long or too heavy. A few dollars getting a stock cut down to fit and a soft recoil pad installed is money well spent. There's nothing you can't do with a pump shotgun, and most hunters in the United States either started out with one or have a couple in their closet.

Much of the rest of our advice is the same for kids as it is for older shooters: Consider lessons with a qualified instructor. Determine eye dominance right out of the gate. Start on an easy outgoing target or floating incoming target. Shoot only one target at a time, and load only one shell at a time. Gradually introduce more difficult shots. If the child is safe, having fun, and wants to shoot, it becomes a lot easier. Soon enough, they'll be ready to hunt.

GOING TO THE FIELD

We highly recommend a hunter's safety course for all new hunters, even if it's not required by your state. In most cases, you can find one by contacting your state natural resources agency. Sometimes, courses are available online, but consider attending one in person with your child. It's a good way to underscore the importance of safety—and who knows, you might learn something as well.

With that done, and a license in hand, it's time for a child's first hunt. Your goal is to make the hunt safe, fun, and memorable for the child—it's not about you. In fact, you probably may want to leave your gun at home. Let the child have all the opportunities, and you may have a hunting partner for life. That's an easy trade-off.

Here are some good options:

Doves: Most of the time, a dove hunt takes place in warm weather and provides plenty of action, and those are good things for new hunters. Give them one shell at a time, and encourage them to make it count. Make sure you have sunscreen, bug repellent, and plenty of cold drinks and snacks on hand.

Kids love to wander in the woods, whether they're hunting or not.

Ducks and geese: If you're in a good spot on the right day, it'll be memorable. Early-season hunts may be a little bit easier, as the birds are less wary and the weather's likely to be a little more reasonable. Again, keep it to one shell at a time for the child's first couple of hunts. A thermos of hot cocoa and a box of donuts never hurts. If you've got a retriever along, that's a good opportunity to introduce another side of hunting. Take it from us—a kid lights up when her four-footed buddy brings back a duck!

Duck hunting can be fun for the whole family.

119

Turkeys: Use a blind to hide any movement. It's hard enough for an adult to sit still, but it's nearly impossible for an excited youngster. Later, you can follow Will's example and sit with your back against a tree, taking in the sights and sounds of nature while waiting for a turkey.

Upland hunting: You may have to wait until the child is a bit bigger and stronger and has more experience before letting them walk with a loaded shotgun. If you can afford it, it's a good idea to start at one of the country's many hunting preserves—the walking is generally easier, there are guaranteed opportunities to shoot, the dog work is usually pretty good, and it's a controlled environment. Walk behind your child, keeping an eye on their gun handling. Tell them when the dog is working bird scent, and remind them to keep the safety on until they mount the gun to fire and to put the safety back on after the shot.

GOLDEN RULES

Kids have a short attention span, but they still want to be successful, like anyone else. Help them do that early on by taking them out on days when you know the doves will be there, when the ducks will be flying, or when the deer are showing up at the same time every day on your trail camera.

If at any time a child seems uncomfortable—cold, tired, hungry—end the hunt. It doesn't matter if the ducks are flying or you hear a gobbler on the next ridge. You want the child to enjoy every minute. Once they're hooked and have been on a few hunts, you can start encouraging them to stick it out a bit longer.

Anthony's girls love to go deer hunting, join him at the duck blind, or go bass fishing. The key is action and success during the first few hunts, and then they're hooked.

Spend a little bit more on good equipment rather than relying on ill-fitting hand-me-downs. Keeping your child warm, dry, and comfortable is worth a few more dollars.

Safety is paramount. Any violations must be addressed immediately and firmly.

Anthony's girls love to spend time with him in the deer stand.

Don't forget a camera! While kids always remember their first duck, goose, or deer, a photograph seals the memory for a lifetime. If it's an especially nice specimen, consider bringing it to a taxidermist.

And teach your kids how to cook their game and enjoy it at the table. That can be almost as much fun as hunting, and another way to celebrate your child's success in the field.

CHAPTER 13

LIFE LESSONS

If you take away only one set of concepts from this book, we hope it comes from this chapter. That's why we put it last, in hopes that it will make a final impression on you. The principles outlined here go further than pointing a gun or shooting a duck, though hunting is a superb gateway to learning them. In short, it's a set of reasons as to why we hunt, and one of the main reasons why we partnered up to bring you this book. And if you think about it, these lessons have applications that go far beyond hunting and shooting.

First, let's acknowledge that **hunting is fun**. We surely wouldn't awaken before dawn and slog through muck and mire if it weren't. The memories we build in the field, with our friends and family, stay with us forever.

Hunting brings with it **an appreciation for nature**. For the most part, we hunt in beautiful places and get to watch the world come awake at dawn and settle down at dusk. If you're watchful, you'll see something new every day you spend in the field. A squirrel may scamper over your boot as you huddle in a tree stand, or a bald eagle may pluck a bass from a marsh as you wait for the morning flight of ducks to begin. The songbirds you see may open your eyes to a whole new and rewarding way of enjoying time spent outdoors. The lessons are all around us.

If you hunt, you will learn **patience, persistence, and discipline**. You can't make the ducks fly, and you can't make a dog into a polished hunter overnight. Often you wait, and wait, and wait . . . and nothing happens, except you get to watch nature in all its splendor. But eventually—maybe tomorrow, maybe next week—something will happen that will make all the waiting worthwhile. That's why patience is a virtue, and why discipline pays off with big results.

At times, you'll have to **sacrifice to succeed**. That might mean a day or two brushing blinds when you'd rather be playing golf, or taking the time to go to the range when you'd rather watch a ball game on TV. But if you give up a few things now, you'll reap greater rewards for the future. You might not get what you want right away, but eventually, you might also wind up with what you want the most.

You will come to appreciate **attention to detail**. Things that may seem trivial can make or break your success in the field—a misplaced decoy, a lack of camo on your face, an ill-blown turkey call, or having the wrong ammunition for the task at hand. The more attention you pay to those little things, the better chance you have of making a big success.

Even so, you might do everything right and still not succeed. If you hunt enough, you'll **learn to accept failure and learn from it**. Maybe the ducks just didn't fly that day, or maybe the turkeys weren't gobbling. It happens, and it has nothing to do with what you did or didn't do. Life happens that way, too. We all fail—it's how you handle it that determines your growth and your future success.

You'll become a better judge of **character**, and hopefully some of that will rub off on you. Watch your partners in the field. Do they claim every bird, even if two people shot it? Do they run to the front when the dog starts acting birdy, or do they step back and let everyone take a turn? Do they show up on time, or offer to pay for the gas? People who say "me first" can get tiresome fast, in the field and in the larger world.

Will likes to say there are three types of people in the world:

1. People who are jealous of you when you succeed—avoid them, because they will bring you down.
2. People who don't care whether you succeed—don't spend much time with them, as they will not bring you up.

3. People who want you to succeed and ask nothing in return. These are the people you want to surround yourself with, in the hunting field, in your career, and in your personal life. And try to be one of those people yourself—Anthony and Will certainly are.

Hunting's also a great way to improve your **self-image**. Watch a kid swell with pride as they pick up their first dove, or their satisfaction when their family sits down to an awesome game dinner they helped bring to the table. That satisfaction applies to adults, too. And the better your self-image, the better you will perform in life as well as in the field.

If you're **passionate** about hunting, you will naturally want to get better at it. Same thing goes for your career and personal life—if you are passionate about them, you will not mind making the sacrifices that lead to your success. Will and Anthony are exceptional hunters, but they are also extremely successful in business. Trust them—a similar approach pays off to both.

You might even get better at **setting goals** for yourself. Will likes to quote the Olympic rifle shooter Lanny Bassham, who says you should set a goal big enough to move you to change your habits or attitudes. If it's too small, it will just not be worth it for you to make changes in your life. Think about how you can bring that to your hunting or shooting. Maybe your goal will be simple, like shooting 100 shells a week for two months before dove season, or it may be longer term, such as mastering a single-reed duck call. But unless you set the goal, you won't even get started on your way to achieving it.

And finally: You probably figured this out by now, but we believe strongly that **anything worth doing is worth doing well**. We've all met hunters who say they're just happy to be there and that they don't care whether they get a bird or not. Sometimes they're sincere, but it's a rare hunter who isn't delighted when he or she makes a tough shot or shoots a limit. Developing the ability to take advantage of your opportunities in the field takes some work and practice. We've given you the road map to do that in this book.

Now go have fun. You'll find that working hard toward a goal can be its own reward, but accomplishing that goal is even better.

ACKNOWLEDGMENTS

My parents were incredible. They always encouraged me by telling me I could accomplish anything I set my mind to doing. Thank you, Daddy, for always making sure one of your brothers could take me hunting or fishing when you could not. Thank you for serving in World War II and setting the example of protecting all that so many of us take for granted. Thank you for working your whole life to provide for our family, for drawing the line and toeing the line.

Thank you, Daddy, for the greatest gift you gave me—your devotion and love for Mama—for through that gift, I learned the true meanings of love, forgiveness, sacrifice, and devotion.

Thank you, Mama, for praying for me every day of my life even as you approach your ninety-seventh birthday. And the biggest thank-you of all is for giving me the foundation that would bring me to know Jesus Christ in a personal way and as my teacher and savior. Galatians 5:22–25.

Will Primos

My family was in the hunting business long before I was born. Starting in the 1950s, my grandparents ran the M&M Hunting Lodge, a waterfowl outfitter in Smyrna, Delaware. If it weren't for them, this book probably wouldn't have been written.

My dad went into the business himself, operating M&M Hunting Preserve in Pennsville, New Jersey, so I grew up in a household that was into hunting, fishing, and later, sporting clays. As a small boy, I went deer hunting, duck hunting, and goose hunting with my dad, igniting a passion that remains today. Without my parents' approval and support, I never would have developed that interest, nor gone to work in our family business. So I thank my parents and my grandparents for starting me down that track.

There are others I'd like to thank, starting with my brother, Mike. We've got good duck and goose hunting nearby on the Delaware Bay, but it's not easy. We deal with long boat rides, rough weather, big tides, and lots of mud, so you need a partner you're comfortable with to help you stay safe. Mike's as capable as can be, and we've learned lots about hunting and shooting through all our years together.

Two other good hunting buddies dating back to my youth are Paul Davolos and Chad DiFebo. We've spent untold hours together out on the marsh, and again, we've been in some risky situations that we probably should have avoided. But we always made it back safely, thanks to those three guys.

Dan Carlisle taught me the fundamentals of clay shooting when I was a kid, and those fundamentals are the foundation of the lessons in this book. Dan's superb teaching set me up to become a professional shooter and instructor.

I have my own family now—my wife, Jessica; our three girls, Emma, Amelia, and Maddie; and their baby brother, Ant. Their love and support allow me to continue my shooting career, and they travel with me around the world when they can. When they can't, Jessica holds down the fort at home and works long hours to keep everything on track. I couldn't do it without them, nor would I want to try.

Anthony I. Matarese Jr.

The authors thank Winchester Ammunition and White Flyer Clay Targets for supporting the creation and publication of this book.

ABOUT THE AUTHORS

Anthony I. Matarese Jr. is the first American to win the World English Sporting Clays Championship and the first person to win the sport's four biggest tournaments: the World English, the World FITASC, the National Sporting Clays Association Championship, and the NSCA's US Open. He is the youngest inductee to the National Sporting Clays Association's Hall of Fame.

Will Primos, the vision and voice of the Outdoor Channel's *Primos TRUTH about Hunting* and pioneer of the game-call industry, has been hunting since he was a boy. Primos Hunting produces world-class hunting accessories and products with a focus on deer, turkey, elk, waterfowl, and predators.

Kerry Luft is an award-winning writer and editor, avid bird hunter, and associate instructor in Anthony Matarese's AIM Shooting School.

INDEX

Italicized page numbers refer to photos.

Printed in the USA
CPSIA information can be obtained
at www.ICGtesting.com
CBHW040619110924
14162CB00016B/318